PRAISE FOR
THE BIG PICTURE
AND STEVE WEXLER

You need a license to drive a car, and you should be required to read this book before you use a chart, a graph, or a table in a presentation. It's fun, clear, and useful. Numbers and words are not enough, it's time we got smart about communicating data.

—SETH GODIN, author of *This Is Marketing*

Steve Wexler's graphs are vivid, funny, practical, and highly informative—and so is this book.

—TIM HARFORD, bestselling author of
The Undercover Economist and *The Data Detective*

Steve Wexler has done for data visualization what Dale Carnegie did for the art of making friends and influencing people, and Strunk and White did for writing. *The Big Picture* helps professionals at every level of an organization master the fundamentals and develop better "maps" that lead to better strategies.

—JOHN C. PITTENGER, former SVP of
Corporate Strategy for Koch Industries, Inc.

You need this book. Data visualization is the key to sifting through the onslaught of numbers in our professional lives, and Steve Wexler gives incisive, practical advice on how to derive deeper insight and understanding from data more quickly. With his infectious love of making data accessible, Wexler enables us to see things differently, inspiring us to ask even better questions.

—JON COHEN, Chief Research Officer of SurveyMonkey

Every business leader will benefit from the wisdom in this book. *The Big Picture* is an essential guide that shortens the time it takes to come to a deeper understanding of your data. Leveraging visuals that truly illuminate insights—and avoid misleading representations—helps organizations be more agile in their decision-making. Every business leader I know wants to make better decisions faster. This invaluable tool will get you there.

—KENDALL CROLIUS, President of G100 Next Generation Leadership

If a picture is worth a thousand words, then *The Big Picture* is worth a million dollars. It will enable business leaders to see patterns in data with the least amount of effort, uncovering opportunities and galvanizing action. Indispensable!

—BRAD EPSTEIN, Chief Marketing Officer of Precision Medicine Group

Steve Wexler's passion for reducing the time to the actionable insights is inspiring, and I came away with new tools to transform data into intelligence and impact. *The Big Picture* is a quick read, and Wexler doesn't get bogged down in theory, but instead uses his arsenal of real-life examples to illustrate his points. I will be sharing this book and its many lessons with my entire organization!

—MOLLY SCHMIED, Chief Analytics Officer at the Office of Advancement of The Ohio State University

Illustrated with a vast array of examples and real-world case studies, *The Big Picture* is a practical primer on data visualization designed to help business professionals achieve a clearer comprehension of dashboards and graphs—and how to use them to change minds. Steve Wexler's smart and humorous approach makes for an enlightening and entertaining read.

—COLE NUSSBAUMER KNAFLIC, founder and CEO of storytellingwithdata.com and bestselling author of *Storytelling with Data*

Data analytics is becoming ubiquitous—but to truly be data driven, businesses must embrace a data culture in which analytics are used democratically and holistically. *The Big Picture* offers essential data literacy lessons necessary for informed, intelligent conversations about data.

—ADAM SELIPSKY, President and CEO of Tableau

THE
BIG
PICTURE

THE BIG PICTURE

HOW TO USE DATA
VISUALIZATION TO MAKE BETTER
DECISIONS—*FASTER*

STEVE WEXLER

NEW YORK CHICAGO SAN FRANCISCO ATHENS LONDON
MADRID MEXICO CITY MILAN NEW DELHI
SINGAPORE SYDNEY TORONTO

1 2 3 4 5 6 7 8 9   LCR   26 25 24 23 22 21

ISBN 978-1-260-47352-0
MHID   1-260-47352-X

e-ISBN 978-1-260-47353-7
e-MHID   1-260-47353-8

Library of Congress Cataloging-in-Publication Data

Names: Wexler, Steve, author.
Title: The big picture : how to use data visualization to make better
   decisions—faster / Steve Wexler.
Description: New York : McGraw Hill, [2021] | Includes bibliographical
   references and index.
Identifiers: LCCN 2021003135 (print) | LCCN 2021003136 (ebook) | ISBN
   9781260473520 (paperback) | ISBN 9781260473537 (ebook)
Subjects: LCSH: Management—Statistical methods. | Information
   visualization. | Visual analytics. | Charts, diagrams, etc. | Visual
   communication. | Decision-making—Statistical methods.
Classification: LCC HD30.215 .W49 2020 (print) | LCC HD30.215 (ebook) |
   DDC 658.4/033—dc23
LC record available at https://lccn.loc.gov/2021003135
LC ebook record available at https://lccn.loc.gov/2021003136

McGraw Hill books are available at special quantity discounts to use as premiums and sales promotions or for use in corporate training programs. To contact a representative, please visit the Contact Us pages at www.mhprofessional.com.

To the data visualization community—
for its never-ending generosity and encouragement

CONTENTS

INTRODUCTION

According to *Forbes* we create 2.5 quintillion (that's 2.5 million trillion) bytes of data every day and 90 percent of the data in the world was created in the last two years alone. With that explosion in data, there's never been as great a need to see and understand that data. That's why data visualization skills are in such great demand.

There are hundreds of books you can buy and courses you can take, but they all have one thing in common: they are designed for the people who create charts and dashboards.

This is where *The Big Picture* is different. *The Big Picture* is for the 99 percent of business professionals who don't create data visualizations, but who need to be able to decipher, understand, and see the value of charts and dashboards if they are to survive, let alone thrive, during the never-ending data deluge.

WHY SPREADSHEETS ARE NOT ENOUGH

In my business dashboard workshops, I ask attendees if their clients and stakeholders tell them that, while they appreciate the effort, they prefer to see a cross tab of numbers.

Lots of hands go up. Indeed, I get a big laugh when I show this slide (Figure I.1).

FIGURE I.1 An amalgam of every client who has expressed concern over replacing their beloved spreadsheets with some other way of presenting the data.

Maybe you feel the same way and love cross tabs. You may be extremely comfortable with being able to glean insight from a spreadsheet and wonder why you would need anything else. Or maybe you and your organization have tried creating charts and dashboards, but these initiatives didn't lead to insights faster.

Reconsider your investment in data visualization because, if you don't learn how to use it effectively, your organization is going to miss out on everything from increasing sales and profits to making employees more fulfilled and more productive. And if that isn't reason enough, if you don't develop this ability, your organization is going to be trounced by competitors that *are* fluent in data visualization.

Let's look at three examples that demonstrate the power of data visualization and how it enables confident, informed decision-making. You should be able to draw parallels between these examples and challenges within your own organization.

Example 1: Notice

There's a pivotal scene in the 2019 comedy film *Dolemite Is My Name* in which Rudy Ray Moore (played by Eddie Murphy) decides to finance his own movie using advance royalties from his comedy albums. This is a huge gamble; if it doesn't work, Moore will be in debt to the record company for the rest of his life. Undaunted, Moore makes the movie but cannot find a studio to distribute it. Desperate, he decides to rent a movie theater for a single, late-night perfor-

mance. To his delight, the show sells out, but Moore is still in debt. He needs a distributor to scale his success.

The next scene opens in the office of a sleazy movie producer who had declined to distribute Moore's movie. He opens a copy of *Variety* magazine and looks at a table of box office receipts. He moves his finger through a column of numbers and sees a number (expressed as a percentage) that grabs his attention. We have no idea what this number refers to, but it's something that astounds the producer, so much so that he exclaims, "What the f*ck-ity f*ck?!"

He immediately phones Moore and says he is ready to distribute the film. So, what changed his mind?

Let's see if you can tell. Have a look at the table in Figure I.2. Do you see anything in the last column that is noteworthy? Remember, it's something in that last column that astounded the producer.

Perhaps nothing stands out. Let's add some data visualization. Does anything stand out in Figure I.3?

You should see a clear outlier, and that the longest bar is more than twice the length of any other bar. This practically screams, "You don't want to miss this!"

Data visualization can help us see opportunities faster. It can get us to "What the f*ck-ity f*ck?!" faster.

Weekly Box Office

Film	Distr	Rank	This week	Cities	Theaters	Pop
Zardoz	FOX	6	$645,500	19	50	18%
Tora Tora Tora	FOX	9	$150,000	14	27	43%
The Day of the Dolphin	AVC	2	$925,000	22	87	31%
Song of Norway	CRC	8	$187,700	19	20	45%
Owl and the Pussycat	COL	1	$1,051,428	18	102	41%
Love Story	PAR	5	$727,500	19	23	34%
Get Carter	MGM	10	$130,000	1	29	23%
Five Easy Pieces	COL	11	$82,900	12	16	28%
Dolemite	IND	12	$42,000	1	1	98%
Cinderella Liberty	FOX	4	$818,000	14	50	39%
Brewster McCloud	MGM	7	$192,900	11	29	19%
Blazing Saddles	WB	3	$825,000	23	78	25%

FIGURE I.2 Weekly box office report as a spreadsheet (not real data).

Weekly Box Office

Film	Distr	Rank	This week	Cities	Theaters	
Zardoz	FOX	6	$645,500	19	50	18%
Tora Tora Tora	FOX	9	$150,000	14	27	43%
The Day of the Dolphin	AVC	2	$925,000	22	87	31%
Song of Norway	CRC	8	$187,700	19	20	45%
Owl and the Pussycat	COL	1	$1,051,428	18	102	41%
Love Story	PAR	5	$727,500	19	23	34%
Get Carter	MGM	10	$130,000	1	29	23%
Five Easy Pieces	COL	11	$82,900	12	16	28%
Dolemite	IND	12	$42,000	1	1	98%
Cinderella Liberty	FOX	4	$818,000	14	50	39%
Brewster McCloud	MGM	7	$192,900	11	29	19%
Blazing Saddles	WB	3	$825,000	23	78	25%

FIGURE I.3 Weekly box office report showing a key metric in a bar chart (still not real data).

The Big Picture: Do you see how easily this 98 percent outlier could have been missed? With the cross tab you had to scan through each number, one by one, looking for an outlier. With the bar chart you processed the information instantly without thinking. Your mind is wired to see things like this.

Yes, this was a made-up example, and in business you would probably take more than one metric into account before making an informed decision. But assuming that the *pop* metric was critical, the bar chart certainly made it stand out.

Let's look at two real-world examples.

Example 2: Notice and Communicate

In late March 2020, the governor of New York gave an impassioned plea for help. New York desperately needed medical supplies to treat Covid-19 patients. His briefings often included useful visualizations, but that day he showed a text table with a bunch of numbers (Figure I.4).

These numbers should make whoever is responsible snap to attention, but it's hard to gauge the gap between what New York had and what it needed. This is a case where data visualization would make this massive shortfall much easier to understand. Figure I.5 shows the same data presented on a bar chart with a reference line.

This approach to showing where you are and where you want to be works with virtually any type of data that aims to show progress toward a goal. With this approach in Figure I.5,

Availability of Critical Items as of March 27

Item	Stockpile	From Fed Government	Total needed
Exam Gloves	1,500,000	350,000	45,000,000
Surgical Masks	4,600,000	860,000	30,000,000
N95 Masks	1,200,000	340,000	20,000,000
Protective Gowns and Coveralls	15,000	145,000	20,000,000

FIGURE I.4 New York State stockpile cross tab (State of New York).

Availability of Critical Items as of March 27
NYS Stockpile | From Federal Government | What we need

Item	What we have	Total needed		
Exam Gloves	1,850,000	45,000,000		Needed
Surgical Masks	5,460,000	30,000,000	Needed	
N95 Masks	1,540,000	20,000,000	Needed	
Protective Gowns and Coveralls	160,000	20,000,000	Needed	

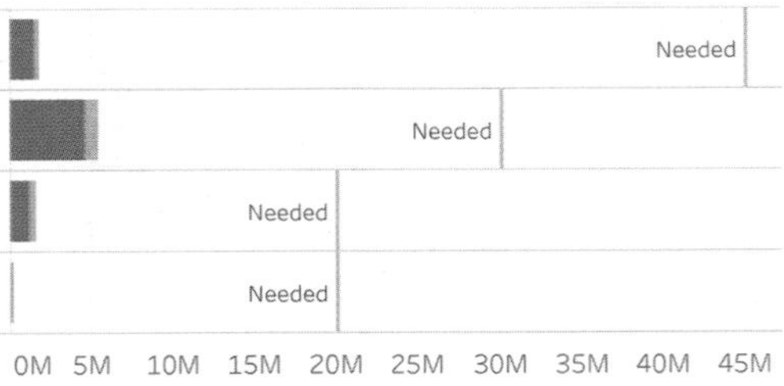

0M 5M 10M 15M 20M 25M 30M 35M 40M 45M

FIGURE I.5 New York State stockpile presented as a stacked bar chart with a reference line.

not only can you see if you are above or below a goal, but you can also see by how *much* you are above or below (and whether you should be celebrating or deeply alarmed).

The Big Picture: You may not be able to count on a marquee presenter to drive your point home. If you have a shortfall that needs immediate attention, the right visualization will help your audience understand (and act) on this urgency.

Example 3: Notice, Communicate, and Persuade

Data visualization isn't just about informing, it's also about persuading.

I was working with a major healthcare company that had data from thousands of organizations about millions of employees. We were creating a campaign to both improve health and reduce costs by getting organizations to make sure employees were compliant with medications and mindful of nutrition. If employees (and their families) kept up with their medications and nutrition plans, they would experience fewer hospitalizations, sick days, and deaths.

Together with sales and marketing, we tried to come up with a way that would get management at these organizations to invest in these initiatives. How could we convince them that this was a serious problem that required a big push to change people's behavior? Showing them a slide like Figure I.6 elicited concerned looks, but no action.

We thought presenting salient facts might resonate (e.g., the organization is ranked 782 out of 790, putting them in the bottom 1 percent), but this didn't strike a chord. We wanted to create a visualization that the audience would feel in their gut that would result in people changing their behavior.

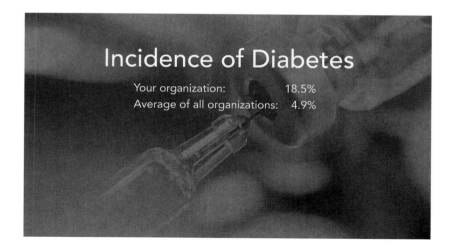

Incidence of Diabetes

Your organization: 18.5%
Average of all organizations: 4.9%

FIGURE I.6
Incidence of diabetes within an organization compared with other organizations. Showing this didn't do anything to change behavior.

After several attempts, we developed a series of charts, starting with the one in Figure I.7.

We made it clear that dots representing organizations at the bottom were doing better than dots at the top.

It's a little difficult to see how many dots there are as they overlap, so we jittered the dots left and right to get a sense of just what 790 looks like (Figure I.8).

Incidence of Diabetes

There are 790 different organizations, each represented by a dot.

Dots near the bottom indicate a low incidence of diabetes; dots near the top indicate a high incidence.

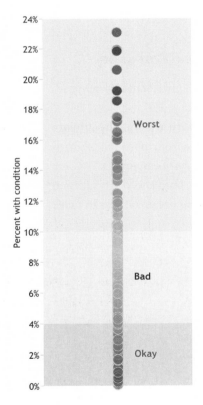

FIGURE I.7 A strip plot showing rate of diabetes among 790 different organizations.

Incidence of Diabetes

There are 790 different organizations, each represented by a dot.

Dots near the bottom indicate a low incidence of diabetes; dots near the top indicate a high incidence.

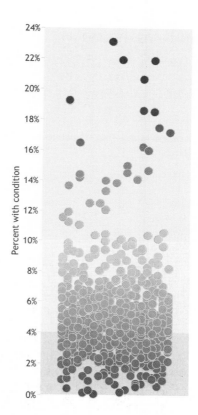

FIGURE I.8 A jitterplot showing rate of diabetes among 790 different organizations.

The position of the dots horizontally doesn't make a difference. We just spread them out so the audience could see how many dots there are. It's now easy to see that most of the dots are clustered toward the bottom.

Next, we added a reference line to show where the worst 1 percent of organizations were (Figure I.9).

We would then show people where their company was among all the dots (Figure I.10).

The reactions were strong and immediate. For the first time, managers could really understand where they stood with respect to other organizations and just what an unenviable outlier they were. These visualizations completely changed how they thought about the data.

The Big Picture: An effective visualization doesn't just help people see things they may have missed; it can motivate people to change

Incidence of Diabetes

There are 790 different organizations, each represented by a dot.

Dots near the bottom indicate a low incidence of diabetes; dots near the top indicate a high incidence.

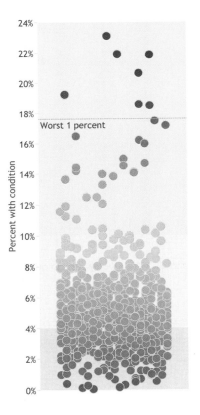

FIGURE I.9 A jitterplot with reference lines showing quartiles and the bottom 1 percent.

Incidence of Diabetes
Your Organization vs. Other Organizations

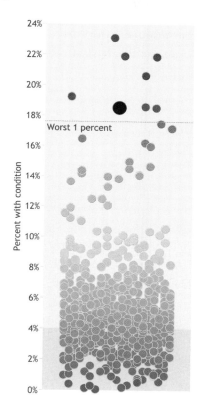

There are 790 different organizations, each represented by a dot.

Dots near the bottom indicate a low incidence of diabetes; dots near the top indicate a high incidence.

FIGURE I.10 A jitterplot highlighting the diabetes rate for a single organization when compared to other organizations. That's a lot of dots—and your dot is one of the worst.

their behavior and, in this case, reduce health-care costs and even save lives.

All three of these examples share one thing in common: they make it much easier to see and understand the underlying data. In the first example, the reaction was, "Look at how much bigger this bar is than all the other bars . . . this could be an amazing opportunity!" In the second it was, "Not only is there a shortfall, but I can *immediately* see how big the shortfall is and understand that we need to move on this, fast." People see the last example and respond with "I knew we weren't doing well, but now I understand the context and can see the degree to which we are underperforming with respect to peer companies, not to mention having our employees at risk. Let's fix this."

WHAT TO EXPECT FROM THIS BOOK

Most organizations are drowning in data but are thirsty for understanding. My goal is to teach you, both quickly and enjoyably, the basics of data visualization so that you and your organization can have informed, intelligent discussions about data. In reading this book you will attain a graphic literacy, or *graphicacy*, that will help you:

- Identify actionable insights
- Accelerate time to action
- Persuade and motivate stakeholders
- Make better decisions—faster

Realize you are not just a mere consumer of charts made by other people; you can drive change in your organization by getting others to see the benefits of graphicacy. Developing this fluency in data visualization is not a boring slog. This stuff is fun! Discovering an insight that was hidden, understanding the true magnitude of

a problem, having an emotional reaction to a chart—all of these make data visualization enthralling.

Guiding Principles for Communicating Data

Here are some considerations for anyone who needs to communicate with data:

- Who is your audience?
- What is important to them?
- What do you want to tell them?
- How can you provide the greatest degree of understanding with the least amount of effort?

That last item is particularly important. It can be tempting, especially to designers, to create slick, eye-catching images that command attention, but if they're difficult to decipher, the benefits of data visualization are lost. When a flashy and confusing chart goes head to head with one that is a little less slick, but straightforward and immediately clear, it's no contest. The chart that's easy to understand wins every time. Clear communication should be the main goal of data visualization *in your organization*.

Notice the phrase *in your organization*. If you look at infographics in a trendy magazine or website, you may think, "That's really cool. Maybe we should be making graphics like that, too."

The Big Picture will focus on *aha* and not *ooh ahh*.

Realize that the designers of these infographics may have emphasized novelty and attractiveness over clarity because they believed they needed to get a reader's attention. I'd argue that the very best designers can create visualizations that are beautiful without sacrificing analytic integrity, but I don't want to go far afield and explore cool graphics for a public audience. I want to focus on reducing the time to insight within *your* organization, which in turn leads to speed to action, and that is why *The Big Picture* will focus on *aha* and not *ooh ahh*.

What Is the Scaredy-Cat?

Although this book is an attempt to celebrate good examples, I'll also show plenty of unhelpful and even misleading examples. I guarantee you will see this kind of work in the wild. In *The Big Book of Dashboards*, my coauthors and I marked these bad examples with the scaredy-cat icon (Figure I.11). While nobody sets out to make bad graphics (except those who are intentionally trying to mislead), I want to make it clear at a glance whether a chart is something you should emulate or avoid.

FIGURE I.11 The scaredy-cat. If you see this icon, it means your organization shouldn't use this type of chart. (Illustration by Eric Kim. Steve Wexler, Jeffrey Shaffer, and Andy Cotgreave, *The Big Book of Dashboards*, John Wiley & Sons. Copyright © 2017 by Steve Wexler, Jeffrey Shaffer, and Andy Cotgreave. All rights reserved.)

A Note on the Coming Attractions

When I introduce a subject in one chapter, I will sometimes make references to it in later chapters. I do this to let you know that I will be discussing it at greater length later, in case you are wondering what chapter will cover it more comprehensively. I don't want you to leave the current chapter you are reading—unless, of course, you want to.

THE
BIG
PICTURE

CHAPTER 1

WHY NUMBERS ARE

NOT ENOUGH

People are not very good at looking at a table full of numbers and being able to derive a lot of insight. Let me prove it to you. Consider this simple spreadsheet that shows 12 months of sales data (Figure 1.1).

Which category has the largest sales, and which has the smallest?

Easy! Just put the totals in a column on the right (Figure 1.2).

But suppose we want to know in which months this was *not* the case? That's a very reasonable question but answering it with this spreadsheet isn't so easy. Looking at the numbers in Figure 1.2, can you see in which months

Sales by Category Over Time

	Jan	Feb	Mar	Apr	May	Jun	Jul	Aug	Sep	Oct	Nov	Dec
Consumer	$256,800	$335,700	$315,000	$337,500	$331,180	$321,000	$179,500	$287,400	$299,500	$310,700	$318,900	$315,000
Corporate	$345,000	$475,000	$245,600	$465,700	$455,000	$476,300	$459,100	$427,800	$456,900	$417,900	$425,000	$521,000
Education	$215,700	$265,400	$183,400	$192,500	$175,800	$209,400	$225,000	$198,600	$201,300	$175,000	$167,200	$168,000

FIGURE 1.1 Sales by category over time as displayed using a spreadsheet.

Sales by Category Over Time

	Jan	Feb	Mar	Apr	May	Jun	Jul	Aug	Sep	Oct	Nov	Dec	Total
Consumer	$256,800	$335,700	$315,000	$337,500	$331,180	$321,000	$179,500	$287,400	$299,500	$310,700	$318,900	$315,000	$3,608,180
Corporate	$345,000	$475,000	$245,600	$465,700	$455,000	$476,300	$459,100	$427,800	$456,900	$417,900	$425,000	$521,000	$5,170,300
Education	$215,700	$265,400	$183,400	$192,500	$175,800	$209,400	$225,000	$198,600	$201,300	$175,000	$167,200	$168,000	$2,377,300

FIGURE 1.2 Sales by category over time, with totals.

Sales by Category Over Time

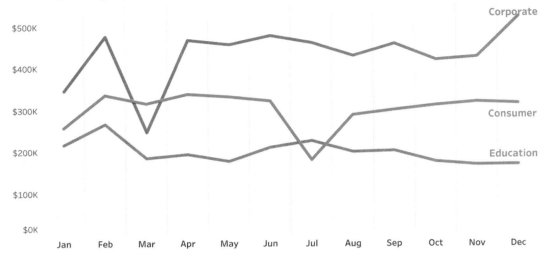

FIGURE 1.3 The same data (sales by category over time) displayed as a line chart. Not only can I see when the top performer category (Corporate) took a dip, but I can also see that the dip was really big.

the Corporate category was not at the top? Now contrast that with how the same data is displayed on a line chart (Figure 1.3).

Seeing the data like this makes it much easier to answer the question about which months bucked the trend. Corporate sales had a big dip in March, and Education sales moved from third place to second place in July.

There's more at work here than just being able to notice things more quickly. On the line chart, there are data points that will draw your attention, but you probably wouldn't notice them on the spreadsheet. A good visualization should both answer questions *and* pose new ones. The line chart will lead me to ask and investigate *why* there were such big dips in Corporate

for March and Consumer for July. Is it cyclical; that is, did it happen in previous years? Should we expect it next year? Is there something we can do to avoid it? Seeing these issues is much harder with just a spreadsheet. I'm not sure I would have thought to ask these questions with a table full of numbers.

> A good visualization can do more than just answer questions; it can help you see that there are other questions you need to answer.

As clear as this example is to me, maybe you are uncomfortable with it and perhaps your stakeholders won't welcome it. You and they may prefer the comfort of seeing every number for every month for every category.

How can I help you and your colleagues see the value of more than just numbers? What's the best way to help people "get" data visualization?

THE "GATEWAY DRUG" TO DATA VISUALIZATION

I want to reassure you and your stakeholders that nobody is going to take away the spreadsheets. I just want to show alternative ways of seeing the data. Indeed, it's easy to create a dashboard that can toggle between a spreadsheet and a line chart, keeping the beloved cross tab just a click away.

But is showing two views the best way to do this, especially if the reluctant adopter tunes out the chart to focus on the cross tab? What might we do to make the cross tab itself more insightful, and at the same time excite people about data visualization?

Here's an example I use to win people over. Consider the spreadsheet in Figure 1.4.

There are four regions and 17 sub-categories, yielding 68 different cells. In which combination of region and sub-category is profit the lowest? Where is it the highest? See if you can find it.

Profit by Region and Sub-category

Product Category	Product Sub-category	Region			
		Central	East	South	West
Furniture	Bookcases	$73	($10,151)	($22,417)	($676)
	Chairs & Chairmats	$37,920	$33,583	$34,026	$44,409
	Office Furnishings	$26,293	$14,523	$25,121	$30,941
	Tables	($19,777)	($50,677)	$26,172	($16,990)
Office Supplies	Appliances	$22,950	$16,812	$26,986	$31,276
	Binders & Accessories	$73,951	$71,420	$69,530	$92,273
	Envelopes	$10,825	$7,482	$19,182	$11,222
	Labels	$2,429	$4,041	$3,479	$3,740
	Paper	$11,047	$13,510	$10,997	$10,433
	Pens & Art Supplies	$2,781	$2,856	$1,397	$518
	Rubber Bands	($174)	($238)	$156	$178
	Scissors, Rulers and Trimmers	($1,765)	($1,179)	($2,903)	($1,953)
	Storage & Organization	($68)	($7,233)	$11,836	($2,018)
Technology	Computer Peripherals	$11,971	$14,808	$30,475	$37,280
	Copiers & Faxes	$513	$67,254	$63,598	$35,997
	Office Machines	$38,876	$47,277	$129,060	$61,377
	Telephones & Communications	$79,393	$73,715	$78,985	$84,860

FIGURE 1.4 Text table showing four regions and 17 sub-categories.

If you answered, "Tables in the East and Office Machines in the South" and you did it in fewer than 10 seconds, bravo! It usually takes most people much longer than that.

Now, let's make one change to make it much easier to find the answers to those questions (Figure 1.5).

In a highlight table, the low values and the high values really pop! In fact, we can glean a lot more than just the best and worst. We can see that Tables are doing poorly in three out of four regions (lots of orange), while Binders & Accessories and Telephones & Communications are doing well everywhere (lots of blue). If you are curious why I used blue and orange hues

and not red and green, it has nothing to do with my being a New York Mets fan. I'll explore why you should avoid red and green in Chapter 3.

The Highlight Table

A highlight table is a combination of a heatmap, in which we use color coding to designate low values and high values, and a text table in which we show the numbers.

I think the highlight table is the gateway drug to data visualization because you haven't taken away the spreadsheet to which some people cling so dearly. You've just augmented it, using color, to make the biggest and smallest

Profit by Region and Sub-category

Product Category	Product Sub-category	Region			
		Central	East	South	West
Furniture	Bookcases	$73	($10,151)	($22,417)	($676)
	Chairs & Chairmats	$37,920	$33,583	$34,026	$44,409
	Office Furnishings	$26,293	$14,523	$25,121	$30,941
	Tables	($19,777)	($50,677)	$26,172	($16,990)
Office Supplies	Appliances	$22,950	$16,812	$26,986	$31,276
	Binders & Accessories	$73,951	$71,420	$69,530	$92,273
	Envelopes	$10,825	$7,482	$19,182	$11,222
	Labels	$2,429	$4,041	$3,479	$3,740
	Paper	$11,047	$13,510	$10,997	$10,433
	Pens & Art Supplies	$2,781	$2,856	$1,397	$518
	Rubber Bands	($174)	($238)	$156	$178
	Scissors, Rulers and Trimmers	($1,765)	($1,179)	($2,903)	($1,953)
	Storage & Organization	($68)	($7,233)	$11,836	($2,018)
Technology	Computer Peripherals	$11,971	$14,808	$30,475	$37,280
	Copiers & Faxes	$513	$67,254	$63,598	$35,997
	Office Machines	$38,876	$47,277	$129,060	$61,377
	Telephones & Communications	$79,393	$73,715	$78,985	$84,860

FIGURE 1.5 The same data rendered using a highlight table.

values really stand out. (Note: You may call a highlight table by a different name. For example, in Excel you can create this type of view using conditional formatting.)

But why stop here? Now that I have your attention, or that of your skeptical stakeholder, let's see how we can add a little something else to the highlight table to add more insight.

The Marginal Histogram

A marginal histogram is a type of bar chart that pairs quite nicely with highlight tables. To see how it works, let's turn to a different example.

Consider a highlight table that shows tech support call volume (Figure 1.6).

Tech Support Calls
By hour and day of week

	Mon	Tue	Wed	Thu	Fri	Sat	Sun
12 AM	109	100	103	115	126	81	100
1 AM	113	79	124	86	104	103	92
2 AM	65	115	133	88	109	100	102
3 AM	66	117	125	112	147	171	81
4 AM	35	142	80	67	130	88	118
5 AM	49	19	72	17	53	6	36
6 AM	6	17	39	9	10	7	4
7 AM	6	1	13	2	9	6	2
8 AM	4	4	6	1	3	2	1
9 AM	23	17	35	4	13	9	19
10 AM	98	115	199	69	104	28	59
11 AM	183	225	226	229	220	208	85
12 PM	241	244	230	333	276	273	204
1 PM	184	210	249	234	221	200	209
2 PM	174	176	239	176	146	125	166
3 PM	116	124	119	126	166	102	117
4 PM	75	104	87	74	110	113	108
5 PM	79	72	98	93	105	77	77
6 PM	69	112	73	84	69	89	112
7 PM	103	92	133	75	82	146	143
8 PM	97	82	97	113	133	143	117
9 PM	104	103	138	83	124	175	102
10 PM	110	107	105	114	132	220	100
11 PM	109	113	108	115	111	142	128

FIGURE 1.6 Tech support calls by day of the week (along the top, going left to right), and hour of the day (left side, going down.)

The darker cells make it easy to see pockets of activity: Thursday at 12 PM is particularly busy. But suppose you want to compare call activity for each *day of the week* and each *hour of the day*, and determine which day has the most calls and which has the least? Or which hour of the day has the most and which the least?

We can get the answers by placing a bar chart along the right side and bottom of the highlight table, as shown here (Figure 1.7).

Tech Support Calls
By hour and day of week

	Mon	Tue	Wed	Thu	Fri	Sat	Sun	
12 AM	109	100	103	115	126	81	100	734
1 AM	113	79	124	86	104	103	92	701
2 AM	65	115	133	88	109	100	102	712
3 AM	66	117	125	112	147	171	81	819
4 AM	35	142	80	67	130	88	118	660
5 AM	49	19	72	17	53	6	36	252
6 AM	6	17	39	9	10	7	4	92
7 AM	6	1	13	2	9	6	2	39
8 AM	4	4	6	1	3	2	1	21
9 AM	23	17	35	4	13	9	19	120
10 AM	98	115	199	69	104	28	59	672
11 AM	183	225	226	229	220	208	85	1,376
12 PM	241	244	230	333	276	273	204	1,801
1 PM	184	210	249	234	221	200	209	1,507
2 PM	174	176	239	176	146	125	166	1,202
3 PM	116	124	119	126	166	102	117	870
4 PM	75	104	87	74	110	113	108	671
5 PM	79	72	98	93	105	77	77	601
6 PM	69	112	73	84	69	89	112	608
7 PM	103	92	133	75	82	146	143	774
8 PM	97	82	97	113	133	143	117	782
9 PM	104	103	138	83	124	175	102	829
10 PM	110	107	105	114	132	220	100	888
11 PM	109	113	108	115	111	142	128	826
	2,218	2,490	2,831	2,419	2,703	2,614	2,282	

FIGURE 1.7 By combining a highlight table with marginal histograms we can both see the big picture and make exact comparisons.

What's a Histogram?

A histogram is a bar chart that shows the distribution of values. In our example 734 calls occurred between 12 AM and 1 AM, 701 between 1 AM and 2 AM, and so on. In a histogram there usually is no space between the bars.*

If you are also wondering why the bars are along the right side and the bottom (and the ones along the bottom are facing down), it was a design consideration. We could certainly put them on the left and along the top but, after experimentation, I thought this looked better. Andy Cotgreave, one of my coauthors on *The Big Book of Dashboards,* calls this hand-wringing about the best way to show the data "axistential angst."

Now we can see that the days with the most calls are Wednesday and Friday (2,831 and 2,703), and the most popular hours are 12 PM and 1 PM (1,801 and 1,507). This is something that would have been very difficult to do without the marginal histograms. Do you see what the trick is for homing in on those dates and times? Just look for the bars that are longer than the others. You'll get the answer considerably faster than trying to compare (and remember) numbers. Try to find the smallest and largest totals in the table in Figure 1.8 and compare that with the bars in Figure 1.7.

---

* In the back of my head, I hear some of my erudite colleagues screaming, "No! A histogram is not a bar chart!" They are technically correct. Histograms plot continuous measures with ranges of the data grouped into bins (which is why the bars often touch, as there aren't supposed to be any breaks), while bar charts compare categorical data. Naomi Robbins wrote a good article about this for *Forbes* that you can find at bigpic.me/histogram.

	Mon	Tue	Wed	Thu	Fri	Sat	Sun	Total
12 AM	109	100	103	115	126	81	100	734
1 AM	113	79	124	86	104	103	92	701
2 AM	65	115	133	88	109	100	102	712
3 AM	66	117	125	112	147	171	81	819
4 AM	35	142	80	67	130	88	118	660
5 AM	49	19	72	17	53	6	36	252
6 AM	6	17	39	9	10	7	4	92
7 AM	6	1	13	2	9	6	2	39
8 AM	4	4	6	1	3	2	1	21
9 AM	23	17	35	4	13	9	19	120
10 AM	98	115	199	69	104	28	59	672
11 AM	183	225	226	229	220	208	85	1,376
12 PM	241	244	230	333	276	273	204	1,801
1 PM	184	210	249	234	221	200	209	1,507
2 PM	174	176	239	176	146	125	166	1,202
3 PM	116	124	119	126	166	102	117	870
4 PM	75	104	87	74	110	113	108	671
5 PM	79	72	98	93	105	77	77	601
6 PM	69	112	73	84	69	89	112	608
7 PM	103	92	133	75	82	146	143	774
8 PM	97	82	97	113	133	143	117	782
9 PM	104	103	138	83	124	175	102	829
10 PM	110	107	105	114	132	220	100	888
11 PM	109	113	108	115	111	142	128	826
Total	2,218	2,490	2,831	2,419	2,703	2,614	2,282	17,557

FIGURE 1.8 Call volume in a text table. This view is not very insightful.

Why Not Just Color Code the Totals?

I can imagine some people may be protesting my example and my claim that the bars are so much better than the text. They might ask, "Why don't you color code the totals the same way you did with the highlight table? Won't that make it easy to see at which hour of the day there are the most calls?"

Sure, let's try that. Consider the highlight table with the totals color coded (Figure 1.9).

	Mon	Tue	Wed	Thu	Fri	Sat	Sun	Total
12 AM	109	100	103	115	126	81	100	734
1 AM	113	79	124	86	104	103	92	701
2 AM	65	115	133	88	109	100	102	712
3 AM	66	117	125	112	147	171	81	819
4 AM	35	142	80	67	130	88	118	660
5 AM	49	19	72	17	53	6	36	252
6 AM	6	17	39	9	10	7	4	92
7 AM	6	1	13	2	9	6	2	39
8 AM	4	4	6	1	3	2	1	21
9 AM	23	17	35	4	13	9	19	120
10 AM	98	115	199	69	104	28	59	672
11 AM	183	225	226	229	220	208	85	1,376
12 PM	241	244	230	333	276	273	204	1,801
1 PM	184	210	249	234	221	200	209	1,507
2 PM	174	176	239	176	146	125	166	1,202
3 PM	116	124	119	126	166	102	117	870
4 PM	75	104	87	74	110	113	108	671
5 PM	79	72	98	93	105	77	77	601
6 PM	69	112	73	84	69	89	112	608
7 PM	103	92	133	75	82	146	143	774
8 PM	97	82	97	113	133	143	117	782
9 PM	104	103	138	83	124	175	102	829
10 PM	110	107	105	114	132	220	100	888
11 PM	109	113	108	115	111	142	128	826

FIGURE 1.9 Highlight table with totals color coded.

One problem is that, because the totals for each row are so much larger than the individual cell values, the color coding within the body of the table isn't as useful. But the bars are valuable for so much more than allowing for nice color coding. Let's look at the totals for 10 AM and 11 AM (Figure 1.10).

10 AM	672
11 AM	1,376

FIGURE 1.10 Comparing two values in a highlight table. We can make an accurate quantitative comparison because the numbers are shown.

10 AM	
11 AM	

FIGURE 1.11 Comparing two values using only color is very difficult.

10 AM	672
11 AM	1,376

FIGURE 1.12 Comparing two values using a bar chart, with labels visible.

10 AM	
11 AM	

FIGURE 1.13 Comparing two values using a bar chart, no labels.

If I were to ask you how much bigger 11 AM is than 10 AM you'd be able to answer, "Easy! It's about twice as big." If I asked you how you knew that you would say, "I looked at the numbers and 1,376 is about twice as big as 672."

Fair enough. Now, let's remove the numbers (Figure 1.11). Can you tell how much bigger 11 AM is than 10 AM?

Yes, we can see that 11 AM is *darker*, but I don't know anyone on the planet who can say 11 AM is twice as orange as 10 AM. Color is great for making it easy to discern differences because we can perceive very slight differences in color intensity, but we cannot easily quantify those differences.

Now, let's see how we do with the length of bars. Let's look at the same two time periods but using a bar chart (Figure 1.12).

Let's see what happens when we remove the numbers next to the two bars (Figure 1.13).

Even without the numbers it's easy to see that 11 AM is about twice as big as 10 AM. Incidentally, this is a really good test of how effective your data visualizations are: can you remove all or most of the numbers and still understand the visualization and make comparisons?

A good test of how effective your data visualizations are: can you remove all or most of the numbers and still understand the visualization and make comparisons?

The ability to make accurate comparisons with bar charts goes away if you have extreme values. You're not going to be able to tell if a bar is 18 times as long as another bar versus 21.5 times as long. But the bar chart is still very valuable in extreme cases because many people can easily see that one bar is way longer than another. (We'll see an example of extreme values and how a good visualization can elicit an emotional reaction in Chapter 9.)

Now, I don't want you to come away from this exercise and think, "Bars, good; color, bad" because color was clearly helpful in making sense of the mass of numbers in the highlight table and it will be an essential ally in your data visualization journey. Color just isn't great for making accurate comparisons. As Charles Minard, one of the great pioneers of data visualization, wrote in 1861: "We can say that one shade is darker than another; that is obvious. But to say that it is two or three times as dark is not visible, it is not readable."*

I'm a big fan of marginal histograms and always look to see if they will add insight to highlight tables and scatterplots. (We'll discuss scatterplots in Chapter 4.)

So, where are we now? We've taken the spreadsheet that our stakeholders (and perhaps you) like so much and enhanced it with useful color coding and simple bar charts. My hope is that this will fuel enthusiasm for what thoughtful data visualization can do to make it easier and faster to glean insights from your data. And with luck, we will get you and your stakeholders hooked on bar charts. After all, you are likely to see a lot of them—and for good reason.

We'll explore why we see so many bar charts in the next chapter.

---

* From RJ Andrews's translation of Minard's treatise *On Graphic Tables and Figurative Maps*. (See https://infowetrust .com/project/minard1861.) When Minard said this, he was looking at a shaded map from 1827 that showed the prevalence of crime in different regions of France. We will explore one of Minard's most famous charts in Chapter 8.

CHAPTER 2

WHY DO WE SEE SO MANY BAR CHARTS?

In the previous chapter we saw how color and bar length helped you better understand data. Color and length are examples of *preattentive attributes*. A preattentive attribute is a fancy term for things that people notice without even noticing they've noticed them; that is, things the mind processes instantly without conscious effort.

Size is another preattentive attribute (Figure 2.1).

It's obvious that the circle on the left is the largest and the one on the right is the smallest, but can we determine how much larger the circle on the left is than the one in the center and the one on the right?

Let's see how color, length, and size stack up against each other in helping people understand the data shown in Figure 2.2.

FIGURE 2.1 Circle size can be used to encode data.

Sales by Category

Phones	$1,127,198
Chairs	$1,022,757
Copiers	$1,007,801
Bookcases	$986,513
Storage	$740,262
Appliances	$677,678
Machines	$508,127
Accessories	$498,533
Tables	$490,011
Binders	$317,245
Furnishings	$256,244
Art	$246,969
Supplies	$162,604
Paper	$161,464
Envelopes	$115,422

FIGURE 2.2 Sales by category sorted from most to least.

We've already seen that bar length does a better job than color when we want to make accurate comparisons. Let's see what happens when the data is encoded with circles of different sizes, called *packed bubbles* (Figure 2.3).

The comparison isn't so easy. For example, if the numbers were not present, could you tell how much larger sales were for Chairs than Accessories? Now let's see what the data looks like using a bar chart (Figure 2.4).

With the bars, it's easy to compare values, but let's see what happens if we use both packed bubbles *and* color (Figure 2.5).

Wow, that certainly grabs one's attention, but is it useful?

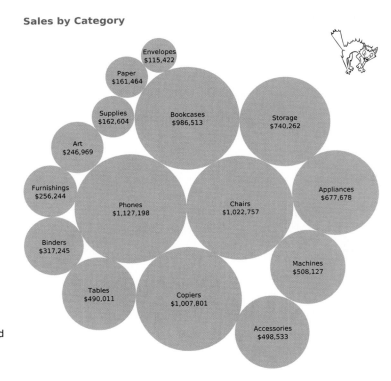

Sales by Category

FIGURE 2.3 Data encoded using packed bubbles.

Sales by Category

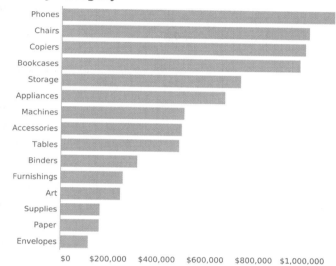

FIGURE 2.4 Data encoded using a bar chart.

Sales by Category

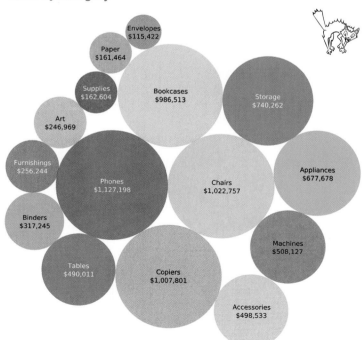

FIGURE 2.5 Data encoded using circle size and color.

Let's put this colorful visualization side by side with the bar chart and see which is easier to use when answering the following questions (Figure 2.6):

- Which category is the third highest?

- Which category is the third lowest?

- Roughly how much larger is the top category (Phones) than the seventh-largest category (Machines)?

The vast majority of people find it easier to answer these questions with the bar chart. We'll discuss why this is in a moment.

PREATTENTIVE ATTRIBUTES

We've just seen three different preattentive attributes at work: color, size, and length. Figure 2.7 shows 10 preattentive attributes that are commonly used in data visualization.

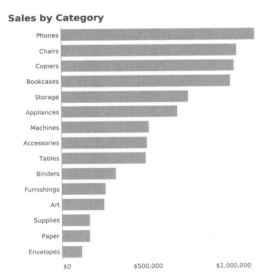

FIGURE 2.6 Comparing a packed bubble chart with a bar chart.

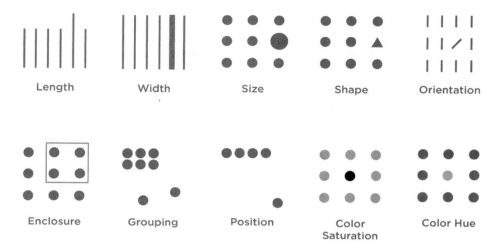

FIGURE 2.7 Preattentive attributes.

You may be wondering, "Which ones are best?"

No single preattentive attribute is best. Each is good for different things, as we will see in various examples throughout the book.

I do, however, want to underscore just how good humans are at comparing the length of bars (or the position of dots) from a common baseline. Humans are amazing at this, even without training.

There's another very potent preattentive attribute that I cannot easily share in a printed book, and that is motion/animation. We'll explore some data visualization examples that use animation in later chapters.

Let me ask you to participate in a simple experiment. Consider the two charts below. Take half a minute and see if you can determine the size (area) of Circle G relative to Circle F, and Bar C relative to Bar A (Figure 2.8).

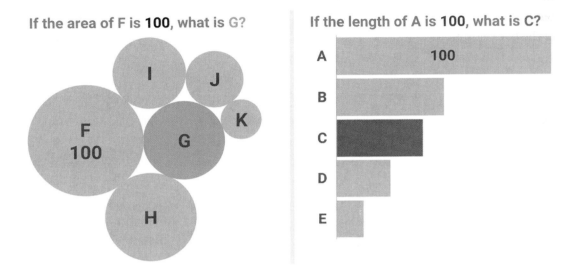

FIGURE 2.8 Try to guess the area of the green circle and length of the blue bar.

The green circle is 50 and the blue bar is 40.

How did you do? If you got the circle correct, bravo. Most people don't. I've done this experiment with more than 2,000 people, and Figure 2.9 shows the results.

Only 42 percent of participants were able to accurately estimate the size of the circle, but almost 80 percent of people got the length of the bar correct. Note the wide distribution of guesses for the circle. Estimates are all over the place and, in fact, more people (43 percent, when you add up all the higher values) *overestimated* the size of the circle. Compare this with the much tighter estimates for the bars. The results are irrefutable: people are much better at *comparing the length of bars from a common baseline* than they are at comparing the area of circles. (I'll explain the italics in a moment.)

Circles and Bars: The Results
Responses: 2,354 ⑦

The circle is 50. Here are the guesses.

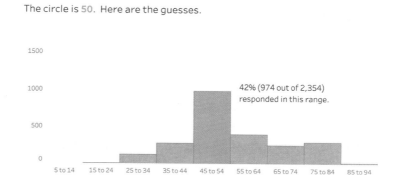

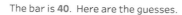

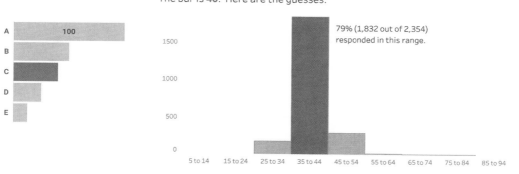

FIGURE 2.9 Responses of people comparing data presented in bars and packed bubbles.

> People are much better at comparing the length of bars than they are at comparing the area of circles.

I also asked people which was harder, estimating the area of the circle or the length of the bar, and 96 percent of respondents reported estimating the circle size was harder.

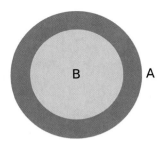

FIGURE 2.11 Comparing the area of two concentric circles.

How Do the Preattentive Attributes Stack Up?

Let's look at how bar length, circle size, and color stack up when trying to make the same comparisons. Here are three different ways to depict two values (A = 80 and B = 40). Let's start with a bar chart (Figure 2.10.)

FIGURE 2.10 Comparing the length of two bars.

It's readily apparent to most people that A is twice as long as B.

Now let's look at two concentric circles (Figure 2.11).

I first saw this example in 2018, when Matthew Kay, a professor at the University of Michigan School of Information, used it. Since then, I've presented it over 100 times and it always freaks me out. The smaller circle is *half* the size

of the larger circle, but most people think it's three-quarters the size. This is because people are much better at comparing length than they are at comparing area. It's also why many people don't realize you get more pizza when you order one 18-inch pie instead of two 12-inch pies.

Finally, let's look at two different shades of blue (Figure 2.12).

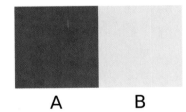

FIGURE 2.12 Comparing the "blueness" of two squares.

I don't know anyone who can look at this and say, "Square A is *twice* as blue as square B." It's difficult, if not impossible, to make accurate comparisons based on color alone.

WAIT! CIRCLES ARE STILL GOOD!

I remember someone in a workshop commenting, "So bars are good, and circles are bad." I was glad they said something rather than silently taking notes because circles can be very useful. They're just not very good if you want to make accurate comparisons.

Consider Figure 2.13, which shows circles on a map.

I ask workshop attendees, "What am I trying to show with this map?" There's often some wiseacre who answers, "The United States." Yes, that's true, but what *about* the United States am I trying to show?

Population?

That's almost always the first answer as people see the really large blob for California, but then realize that if it were population, then the blobs for Oregon and Washington (also on the West Coast) would not be so large.

Electoral college?

No, that relates directly to population.

Rainfall?

Good answer. What else might it be?

Recreational use of marijuana?

Excellent guess, but if that were the case the blob for Colorado would be larger.

FIGURE 2.13 Mystery map: what do the circles encode?

Number of startups?

Could be.

I then reveal that I have *no idea* what this chart shows. I made it years earlier and forgot to include a title.

Whatever this map is trying to show, we can see that there's way more of it happening on the West Coast—and that is useful! While we can't make precise comparisons, the map gives us a very helpful overview, and, if we combined this with a bar chart on a dashboard, we could determine whatever the big picture is *and* be able to derive accurate comparisons.

COMPARING BARS FROM A COMMON BASELINE

I promised I would address the idea that it's easy to compare the length of bars *from a common baseline*. Just what do I mean by that?

Have a look at the four bars in Figure 2.14. Can you sort them from largest to smallest?

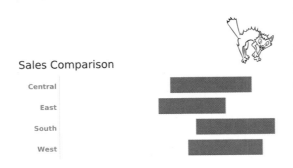

Sales Comparison

FIGURE 2.14 A floating bar chart.

Unless you have a ruler handy, sorting these floating bars is exceedingly difficult. Now let's see what happens when we present them so they start from a common baseline (Figure 2.15).

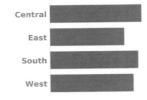

Sales Comparison

FIGURE 2.15 Bar chart with a common baseline.

Now it's much easier. The answer is: Central, South, West, East.

You may be thinking, "When would I ever have to compare the length of floating bars?" In business communication, stacked bar charts come up all the time, and they often use floating bars. (We'll explore this in depth in Chapter 4.)

There's something else to keep in mind about the importance of a common baseline in bar charts. For many people, this is a commandment in data visualization: thou shalt *not* start bar charts from any old baseline. The next section looks at the dangers of breaking this rule.

Beware of the Value Axis Not Starting at Zero

Consider the chart shown in Figure 2.16.

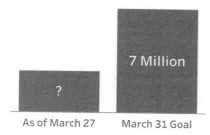

FIGURE 2.16 Can you guess the number represented by the bar on the left?

If the bar on the right is 7 million, try to estimate the number represented by the bar on the left. It should be easy to see that the bar is less than half so we know it will be less than 3.5 million. So maybe 3 million? 2.5 million?

Those are good guesses. With that in mind, what should we make of this graphic that appeared on a major news network in 2014 (Figure 2.17)?

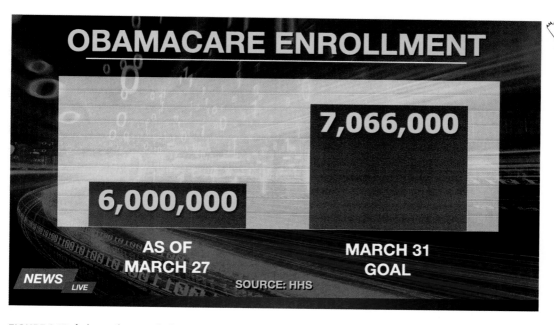

FIGURE 2.17 A deceptive graph that appeared on a major news network on March 27, 2014 (data from the Department of Health and Human Services, graphic reenactment by Randy Krum).

This is an example of not only a *scaredy-cat* but also a TURD (a truly unfortunate representation of data).* Readers need to recognize how this type of representation distorts the data.

The bar on the right is a lot bigger than the one on the left, but the numbers don't reflect this. If the lengths of the bars are correct, then the data should reflect the values in either Figure 2.18 . . .

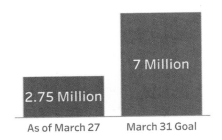

FIGURE 2.18 One version of the graph where the numbers match the bar length shown in Figure 2.17.

. . . or the values in Figure 2.19.

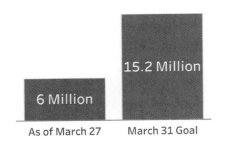

FIGURE 2.19 Another set of numbers that would go with the bars shown in Figure 2.17.

Conversely, if the numbers are correct, then the bars must be wrong. Indeed, Figure 2.20 contains a chart that would accurately reflect the numbers 6,000,000 and 7,066,000 from the news network's chart.

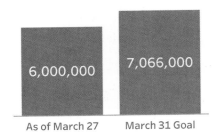

FIGURE 2.20 A chart that shows the bar length corrected to align with the values.

Do you see why the news network's graphic is so misleading? Imagine if I were to say, "You know that thing you are innately good at: comparing the length of bars from a common baseline? Well, I want you to ignore that completely and instead focus on something you are bad at doing, which is trying to envision magnitude just by looking at numbers." That is what this graphic asks you to do.

The news network's chart violates one of the sacrosanct rules of data visualization because it does *not* use a common baseline. In other words, the y-axis does *not* start at zero (Figure 2.21).

* Math educator and author Christopher Danielson came up with this clever acronym in 2011.

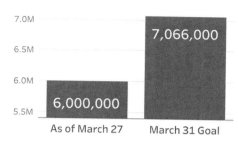

FIGURE 2.21 In this chart the y-axis starts at just under 5.5 million. The common baseline starts further down and isn't visible.

So, just where is the common baseline that is so useful for accurately comparing the length of bars? It isn't visible in the chart above, but you can get an idea of where it is in Figure 2.22.

FIGURE 2.22 What we miss when we truncate the axis of a chart and show only the tip of the data iceberg.

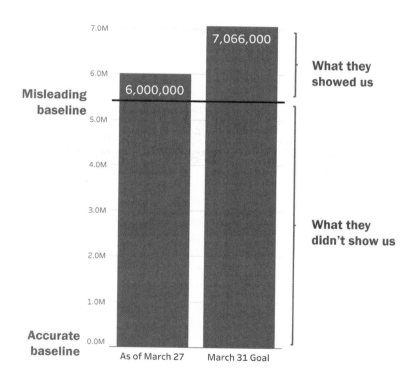

Is it ever OK to not have the value start at zero?

Yes, although probably not for a bar chart. We will explore this in Chapter 4.

If you are still not convinced that a non-zero y-axis is a problem, maybe the pictogram in Figure 2.23 will change your mind.

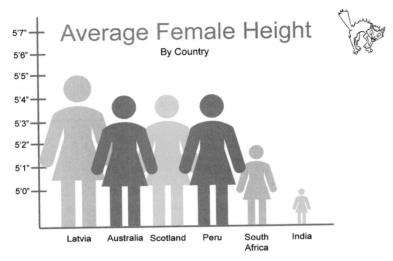

FIGURE 2.23 A pictogram comparing the average height of women from several countries. A version of this graphic went viral when Sabah Ibrahim tweeted, "As an Indian woman, I can confirm that too much of my time is spent hiding behind a rock praying the terrifying gang of international giant ladies and their Latvian general don't find me" (see bigpic.me/viral).

We've looked at bars, circles, and color. Before we get into some of the chart types you should be familiar with, there's more we need to understand about color. We'll look at that in the next chapter.

CHAPTER 3

HOW AND WHEN TO USE COLOR

As you become a more informed consumer of data visualizations, you may start to chime in when you see things you think would help present data more clearly. Good. Your organization will benefit as you advocate for clarity and become a *patron of the charts*.

In your discussions with colleagues, you may run into people who have good intentions but bad ideas when it comes to color. Their ideas may sound an awful lot like, "This dashboard is dull and needs to have more impact. More colors and bolder colors would help a lot."

This is probably bad advice. (Recall how the colored packed bubbles in Figure 2.5 didn't help.) Here are some examples and recommendations that will help you see what works and what doesn't with color in data visualization.

THE FIVE WAYS TO USE COLOR

Here's a graphic based on one that my colleague Jeffrey Shaffer created for *The Big Book of Dashboards*. We joke that if you understand this graphic, you understand everything there is to know about color in data visualization (Figure 3.1).

Color Use in Data Visualization

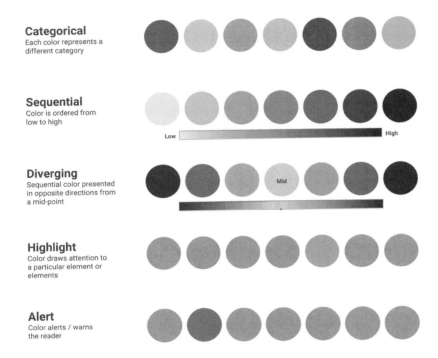

Categorical
Each color represents a
different category

Sequential
Color is ordered from
low to high

Low   High

Diverging
Sequential color presented
in opposite directions from
a mid-point

Mid

Highlight
Color draws attention to
a particular element or
elements

Alert
Color alerts / warns
the reader

FIGURE 3.1 Everything you need to know about color in one simple graphic.

This may be an oversimplification, but this graphic does encapsulate every way you can use color in data visualization.

Categorical Color

Let's focus first on categorical color, which is where most people go astray.

Here are some examples:

- Your company has eight divisions, and you use a different color to identify each division.

- Your school system has 18 districts, and you use a color to differentiate each district.

- The part of the world you are studying has 34 countries, and you differentiate each country using a distinct color.

Why won't this work?

Let's apply categorical coloring to the 34 countries in Asia (Figure 3.2).

The Countries of Asia

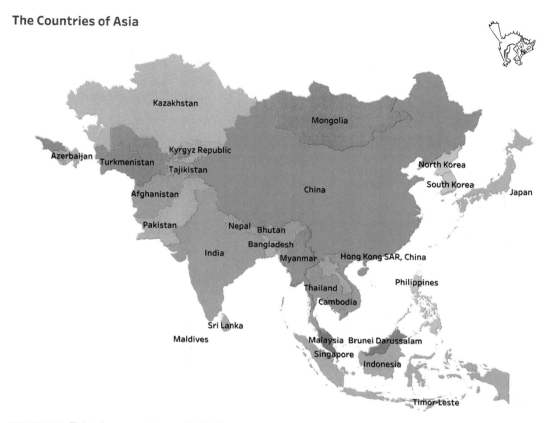

FIGURE 3.2 Thirty-four countries and 34 different colors.

How does categorical color help us understand the data? In this case, having 34 different colors doesn't do anything useful besides making it possible to see the demarcation among the different countries (something you could do with one color and a border around each country).

While the idea of using 34 colors because you have 34 countries is bad, categorical color on a map can be helpful in certain situations.

Consider the example in Figure 3.3, which shows the 34 countries of Asia color coded by the different divisions of a sports tournament. This is a good use of categorical color.

How many categorical colors are too many? There's no rule, but flags go up for me if there are more than four. We'll explore this a little later, but first let's explore sequential and diverging color.

Sequential Color

Suppose instead of coloring categorically, we color by a measure (e.g., wealth, population, average family size, etc.). This is where sequential color comes in; you use different shades of the same color to reflect the measure you are trying to show. Let's explore female life expectancy in Asia using sequential color (Figure 3.4).

Asian Sports Tournament

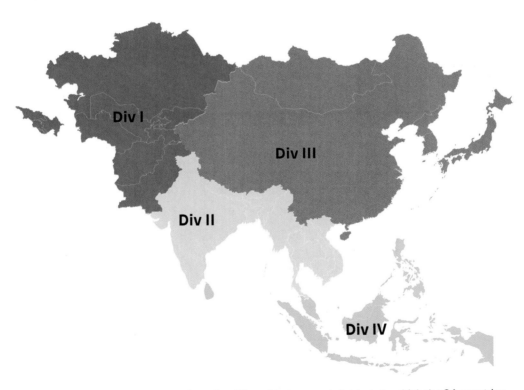

FIGURE 3.3 Using categorical color to show the different tournament divisions to which the 34 countries in Asia belong.

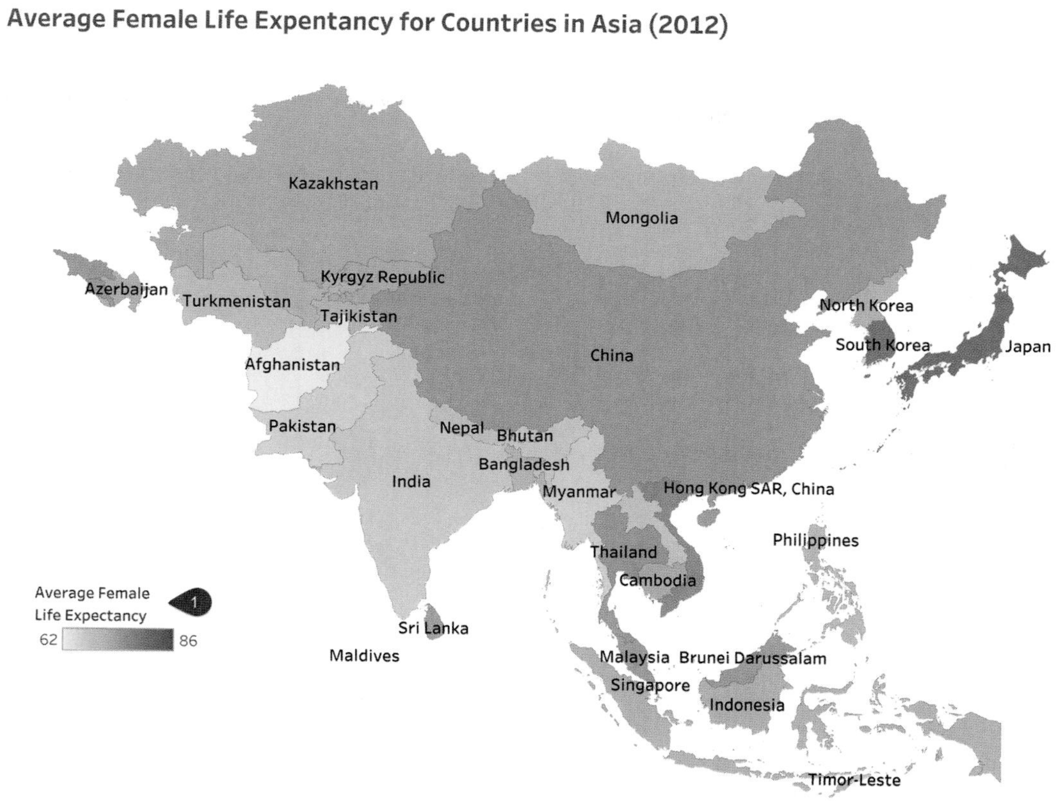

Average Female Life Expentancy for Countries in Asia (2012)

FIGURE 3.4 A sequential color palette to compare female life expectancy in Asia (data from the World Bank).

Look at Japan, where we see dark blue (indicating longer life expectancy), and compare this with Afghanistan, where we see the lightest blue (indicating shorter life expectancy). Using sequential color here helps us see patterns in the data.

Just how much longer and shorter are the life expectancies in these two countries? To answer this question we need a color legend, which is presented toward the bottom left (1), that shows the two extreme values.

Sequential color works when you want to show low to high values using a continuous scale. But suppose you want to see the degree to which something is above or below a logical mid-point (e.g., average unemployment rate)? This is where a diverging color palette works best.

Diverging Color

We use a diverging color palette when we want to show values that are above and below a mid-point. For example, imagine a company wants to show in which states they generated a positive profit and in which they faced a loss (Figure 3.5).

In this example it's easy to see that California and New York are very profitable, and Texas is very unprofitable.

Take a look at the legend and note that the mid-point does not have to be zero. Let's reconsider our female life expectancy map and instead color code it to show which countries have longer and shorter life expectancies when compared to the average of the entire continent, where the average is 74.6 years (Figure 3.6).

Profit by State

FIGURE 3.5 Color coding indicating how profitable each state is for a company. Notice the color legend in the upper right, which shows the extreme values.

In which Asian countries is female life expectancy longer and shorter than average? (2012)

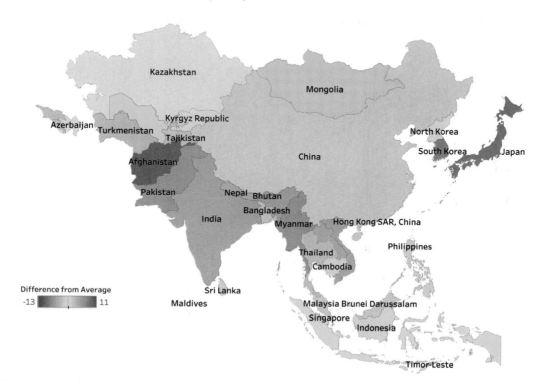

FIGURE 3.6 Using diverging color to show which countries have longer and shorter life expectancies when compared to the average for the entire region (data from the World Bank).

Countries in blue have life expectancies that are higher than average, and those in orange have life expectancies that are lower than average.

Highlight and Alert Colors

Highlight and alert colors are special cases of categorical color. You use them to instantly draw attention to something you want people to notice.

In Figure 3.7, we use a highlight color to draw your attention to Kazakhstan and Pakistan.

The designer will do this because he or she believes that there is something about these two countries that will interest the audience.

Indeed, this approach is showcased in Figure 3.8, where we see a portion of a dashboard that has been customized to highlight the product categories that the user manages.

There are two countries **that I want you to notice.**

FIGURE 3.7 Using a highlight color to make two countries stand out.

Sales by Product Category
Categories You Manage

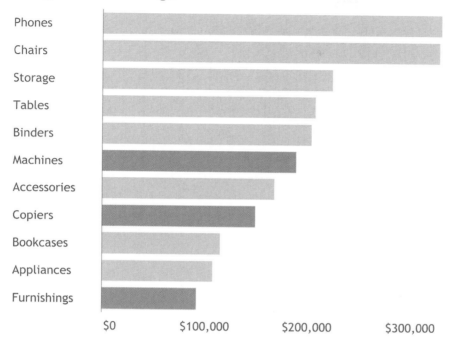

FIGURE 3.8 Using blue to highlight the product categories that are important to the audience.

An alert color works like a highlight color, but takes certain cultural assumptions into account as the goal is not just to highlight, but to suggest there may be a cause for concern.

In Western culture, red is often associated with warning, danger, financial losses, and so on, so some visualization designers will use it not only to highlight data, but also to indicate to the audience that it is undesirable. For example, Figure 3.9 uses red to show which stores have not met their quota.

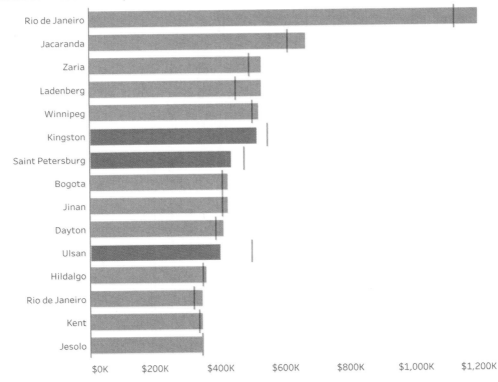

Sales by Store Location (| = Goal)
Meets or Exceeds Goal | Below Goal

FIGURE 3.9 Using red to alert the user to the stores that are not meeting their goals.

This notion that red equals bad can be hard to shake. In Western culture we grow up with these associations:

- Stock market: Green is up; red is down.

- Traffic lights: Green means go; red means stop.

- Finance: We're in the black (yay); we're in the red (boo).

But realize that this is hardly universal. In many Asian nations, the associations with red and green are sometimes reversed. In addition, organizations that have red logos tend to use red to mean something good. Indeed, I've seen the same chart as the one above, but where the red and grays are reversed.

What's your reaction to the following map (Figure 3.10)?

What's up with Mongolia?

FIGURE 3.10 What's going on in Mongolia?

I see it and can't help thinking, "It's red . . . is there a problem there?" But someone in another country (or someone who works in a company with a red logo) may think, "It's red . . . is something good happening there?"

Without any further context, the audience's biases and assumptions will drive the answer.

USE COLOR SPARINGLY

If I could make only one recommendation on how to use data visualization effectively, it would be to use color sparingly.

Rentals by Day of Week

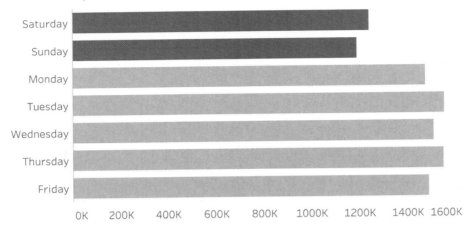

FIGURE 3.11 What the first group sees. Here I use the preattentive attribute of color to draw attention to Saturday and Sunday.

Rentals by Day of Week

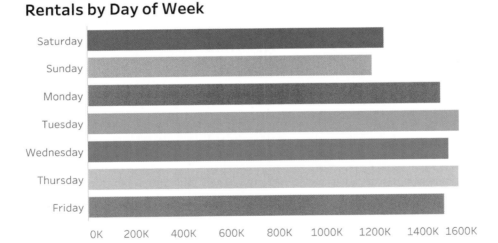

FIGURE 3.12 What the second group sees. Here I use the preattentive attribute of color to confuse people.

Here's an exercise I do in my workshops and presentations. I show half the group the chart in Figure 3.11 for five seconds.

I show the other half of the group the alternative chart in Figure 3.12 for five seconds.

Next, I display a blank screen and ask everyone to open his/her eyes. I ask the first group if there was anyone who was able to draw a conclusion from the image I had shown them. Somebody in that first group will offer, "Rentals on Saturday and Sunday are less than other days." I'll then ask, "How many people in the first group saw that rentals on weekends are less?" *Lots* of hands go up.

I then ask the second group how many people reached the same conclusion. Very few hands go up.

Finally, I show both groups what the other group had seen, assuaging the concerns of the second group that they were somehow less intelligent than the first (Figure 3.13).

Do you see how powerful color is in the first example, and how useless it is in the second? In the second example, you have to fight color to glean any insight.

Using color sparingly and purposefully makes it easier to draw conclusions.

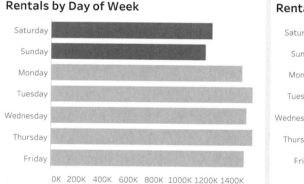

Rentals by Day of Week

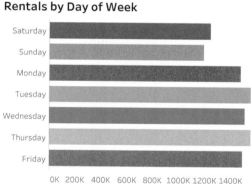

Rentals by Day of Week

FIGURE 3.13 Color on the left highlights something interesting about the data; color on the right obscures any insights about the data.

Let's see how this works and what conclusions you can draw from a few more examples. Figure 3.14 tells us something about Sunday.

Conclusion: The fewest rentals are on Sunday.

Figure 3.15 tells us something about Tuesday.

Conclusion: There are more rentals on Tuesdays than on any other day.

Rentals by Day of Week

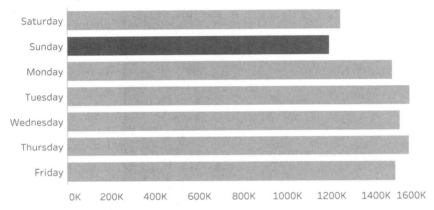

FIGURE 3.14 Sunday rentals are highlighted.

Rentals by Day of Week

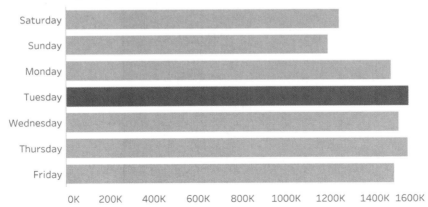

FIGURE 3.15 Tuesday rentals are highlighted.

Figure 3.16 tells us something about Wednesday.

Conclusion: Something is up with Wednesday. I'm not sure what, but because it is red—and because I grew up in a culture in which red is associated with warning/danger—I guess I should be concerned.

What about Figure 3.17? What is that one telling us?

Conclusion: No idea. Is somebody throwing a party?

Rentals by Day of Week

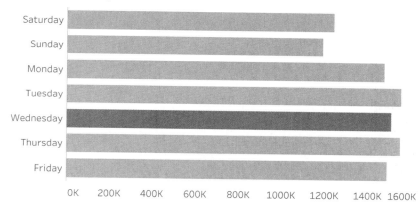

FIGURE 3.16
Wednesday rentals are highlighted in red.

Rentals by Day of Week

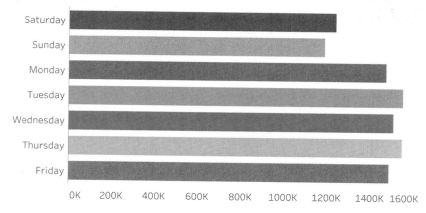

FIGURE 3.17 Using so many colors impedes our ability draw any insights from the data.

Curating Results

Let's go back to the first version in which Saturday and Sunday were in blue and everything else was gray. Yes, I wanted people to see that there was an interesting story about the weekends, but why make the audience work for the *aha*? Why not hit them over the head with it, as we see in Figure 3.18?

I would argue that if this were in a document or slide deck, then yes, curating the results so that your audience does not have to work as hard as you, the content creator, did is warranted.

When and how to curate findings is a little beyond the scope of this book (although we will address it briefly in Chapter 7). The subject is also covered brilliantly in Cole Nussbaumer Knaflic's book *Storytelling with Data*.

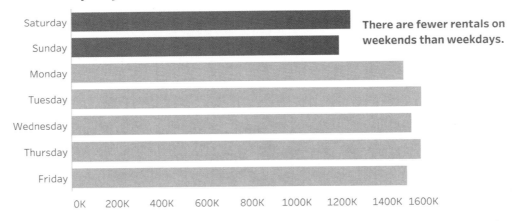

FIGURE 3.18 If this image appears in a curated presentation as opposed to an exploratory dashboard (where we want people to discover things for themselves), why not help them arrive at interesting conclusions we've already drawn?

COLORBLINDNESS

You may be wondering why the diverging color map in Figure 3.6 earlier in this chapter uses blue and orange rather than the "universally accepted" red and green, as shown in Figure 3.19.

My friend and colleague Kelly Martin once said, "There's no way to *un-ugly* red and green,"

but besides aesthetics and cultural considerations, is there a good reason to avoid these colors?

The answer is yes, as roughly 1 in 10 men suffer from some form of red-green colorblindness (also called *color vision deficiency*, *CVD*). The percentage for women is roughly 1 in 100. This means that to a person suffering from red-green

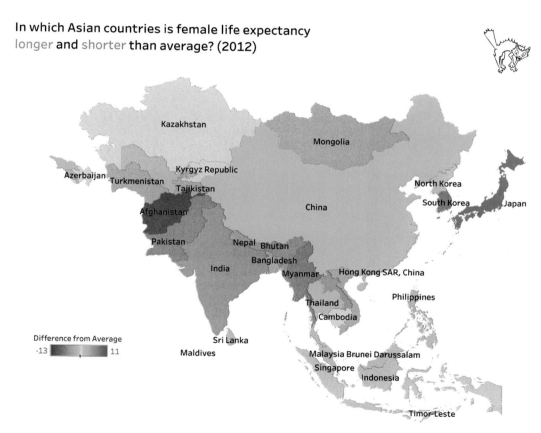

In which Asian countries is female life expectancy longer and shorter than average? (2012)

FIGURE 3.19 Filled map using red-green diverging color (data from the World Bank).

colorblindness, a map using red and green shading will look something like Figure 3.20.

The problem is that both ends of the spectrum (Afghanistan and Japan) look the same!

Data visualization is supposed to make it easier to compare things. What will the 10 percent of your male audience make of this?

If you can, consider using blue and orange.

But what if others in the organization insist on traffic light colors? We suggest you modify them slightly. In *The Big Book of Dashboards*, Jeffrey Shaffer suggests modifying the classic

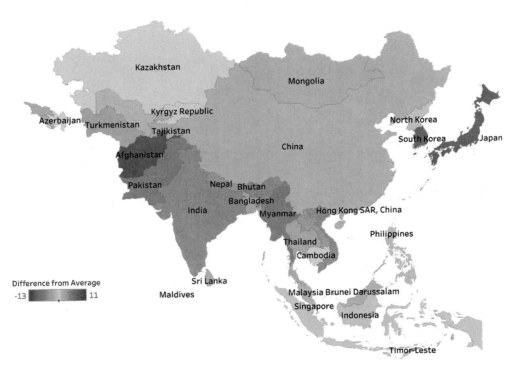

In which Asian countries is female life expectancy longer and shorter than average? (2012)

FIGURE 3.20 Simulation of what a map that uses red and green looks like to someone with deuteranopia, a type of color vision deficiency (data from the World Bank).

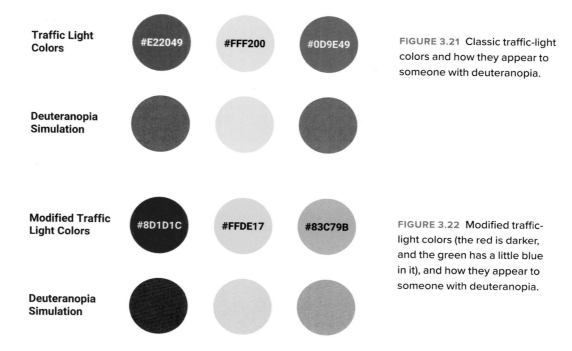

Traffic Light Colors — #E22049, #FFF200, #0D9E49

Deuteranopia Simulation

FIGURE 3.21 Classic traffic-light colors and how they appear to someone with deuteranopia.

Modified Traffic Light Colors — #8D1D1C, #FFDE17, #83C79B

Deuteranopia Simulation

FIGURE 3.22 Modified traffic-light colors (the red is darker, and the green has a little blue in it), and how they appear to someone with deuteranopia.

traffic light color combination, changing them from what's shown in Figure 3.21 to what you see in Figure 3.22.

The colors still read as red, yellow, and green, but they will also work for someone who has red-green CVD.

DO WE EVEN NEED TO USE COLOR?

If we want to get a sense of the big picture or see if countries in proximity to each other have similar tendencies, then the sequential and diverging colors on maps of Asia can be very use-ful, but remember that humans are not very good at making accurate comparisons using just color (we explored this in Chapters 1 and 2). While we can see that some colors are darker than others, it might be better to show the data on either a bar chart or a dot plot, both of which use position from a common baseline to enable comparisons. Take a look at Figure 3.23, which presents the same life-expectancy data as a bar chart.

With a bar chart or a dot plot, it's easy to see which countries have above-average life expec-tancies and which have below-average life ex-pectancies (and by how much). It's much easier for our brains to make the comparisons.

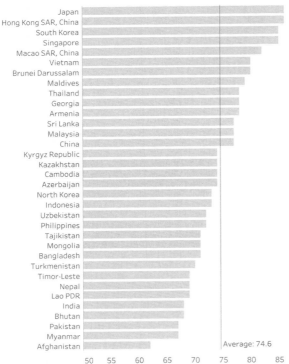

Average Female Life Expectancy for Countries in Asia (2012)

FIGURE 3.23 A bar chart might be a better way to compare the female life expectancy among these 34 countries (data from the World Bank).

Why Not Use Both?

Bar charts and maps have their respective advantages and disadvantages, so why not have a view that employs both? This life expectancy data presents a case in which a dashboard with several charts may be warranted. We'll discuss this at length in Chapter 7.

And just to drive home the point about the gratuitous use of categorical color, observe how adding color makes it harder to understand the chart (Figure 3.24).

CONCLUSION

Use color sparingly and purposefully, and train yourself and your organization to put up warning flags if your visualizations have more than a few

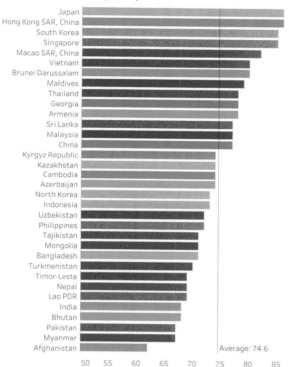

Average Female Life Expectancy for Countries in Asia (2012)

FIGURE 3.24 Adding a different color for each country does not help us understand the data and makes the chart harder to read (data from the World Bank).

categorical colors. When you explore the examples in Chapter 9, you will see that all of the visualizations adhere to these recommendations.

Also, make sure your organization's designers test their images with a CVD simulator. You don't want to instantly alienate 10 percent of your male audience and 1 percent of your female audience who suffer from red-green CVD, nor do you want to alienate the people who suffer from difficulties with less common, but still avoidable, color combinations.

Here are a few recommended color vision deficiency simulators:

• **Chromatic Vision Simulator** (free). Kazunori Asada's superb website allows users to upload images and simulate how they would appear to people with different forms of CVD. Asada also makes a free app for Android and iPhones that allow you to use your phone camera to simulate different forms of CVD. See http://asada.tukusi .ne.jp/webCVS/ and https://asada .website/cvsimulator/e/index.html.

- **Coblis Colorblind Simulator** (free). An excellent CVD simulator that allows you to upload your images and see how they would appear to people with different forms of CVD. See https:// www.color-blindness.com/coblis -color-blindness-simulator/.

- **Adobe Illustrator CC.** This program offers a built-in CVD simulation in the View menu under Proof Setup.

Just one more thing. Take a look at Figure 3.25.

You looked at Vietnam, didn't you?

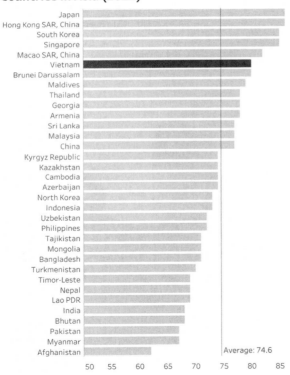

Average Female Life Expectancy for Countries in Asia (2012)

FIGURE 3.25 Even gray scale can be very powerful (data from the World Bank).

CHAPTER 4

WHAT CHARTS
YOU SHOULD KNOW
AND LOVE
(AND SOMETIMES LOATHE)

could easily fill an entire book with hundreds of different chart types and their appropriate uses, but I want to focus specifically on arming you with the chart types that are most useful for communicating business data. The good news is that as you learn how to decode and appreciate these charts, your graphicacy (that's the term for *graphic literacy*) will improve and you'll be better at understanding *any* charts that come your way.

BAR CHARTS AND ALTERNATIVES

We've already looked at examples of highlight tables and bar charts, but there are a few more considerations and variations everyone should know.

Horizontal and Vertical Orientation

Bar charts are particularly versatile in that they can be displayed with either a horizontal or vertical orientation. Figure 4.1 shows an example of a horizontal orientation.

Figure 4.2 displays the same chart vertically. Bar charts with vertical orientation are sometimes called column charts.

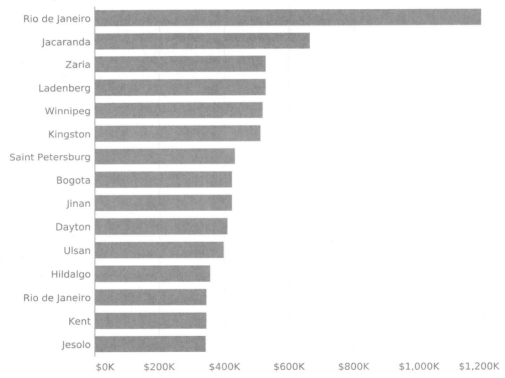

Sales by Store Location

FIGURE 4.1 A bar chart showing sales by store location, sorted from highest to lowest, using horizontal orientation.

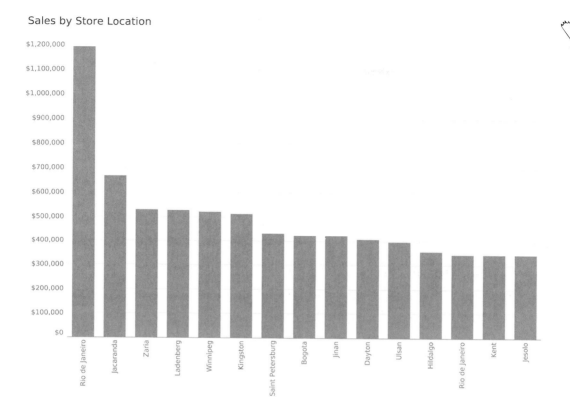

FIGURE 4.2 A bar chart showing sales by store location, sorted from highest to lowest, using vertical orientation.

So why the scaredy-cat? Look at the labels along the x-axis at the bottom. To fit all the letters, we either need to display the text vertically (as we do here) or on a diagonal. Both vertical and diagonal text are hard to read. Sometimes something as simple as turning a bar chart 90 degrees makes it much easier to use. Note that I have no problem with displaying bars vertically, as long as the text labels are easy for the audience to read. In this example, they are not.

Dot Plots and Lollipop Charts

Dashboard designers often get pushback from their stakeholders who tell them that bar charts are boring. I'd argue that the bar charts are fine and it's the data that's boring, but there are some analytically sound and aesthetically pleasing alternatives that you should know about. One alternative is a dot plot, also called a Cleveland plot (Figure 4.3).

The Cleveland plot is named for William Cleveland who worked at Bell Labs. In the early 1980s, he and his colleague Robert McGill published seminal research on how well audiences could estimate values using different charts. Cleveland and McGill's research showed that people make better estimates using *position* from a common baseline than they do guessing the size of circles, the size of a slice in a pie chart, and so on.

Sales by Store Location

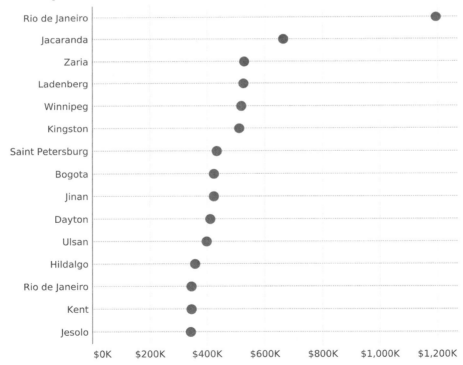

FIGURE 4.3 Sales data displayed using a dot plot, also called a Cleveland plot.

Noticed that I italicized the word *position* as Cleveland and McGill's research shows that people are a little better at judging position than they are at estimating length. This, combined with the dot plot's uncluttered appearance (it uses a *lot* less ink than bars), is why many data visualization experts prefer the Cleveland plot to bar charts.*

Figure 4.4 shows another alternative to the bar chart, the lollipop chart.

Sales by Store Location

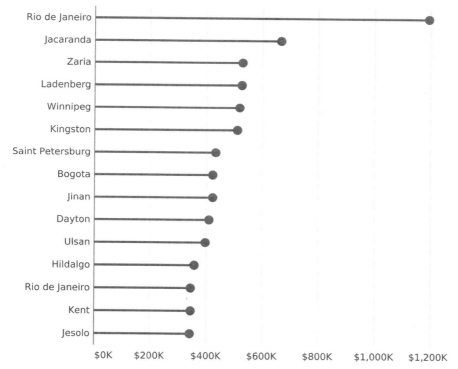

FIGURE 4.4 Sales data displayed using a lollipop chart.

---

* See Cleveland, William S. 1984. "Graphical Methods for Data Presentation: Full Scale Breaks, Dot Charts, and Multibased Logging." *The American Statistician*, 38:270-280, and "Dot Plots: A Useful Alternative to Bar Charts" by Naomi B. Robbins at https://www.perceptualedge.com/articles/b-eye/dot_plots.pdf.

I like both the Cleveland plot and lollipop chart a great deal, but some of my colleagues point out that the circle introduces some imprecision, as it is unclear if you should be comparing the left, center, or right edge of the dot. I will confess that I used to make my lollipop dots larger, and this critique convinced me to make them smaller. You can also ditch the candy portion and replace it with a vertical line at the end (Figure 4.5).

Which of these variations do I think your organization should use? While the designers should strive to find the one that stakeholders find most valuable, I'll be happy if your organization uses *any* of these instead of packed bubbles or pie charts!

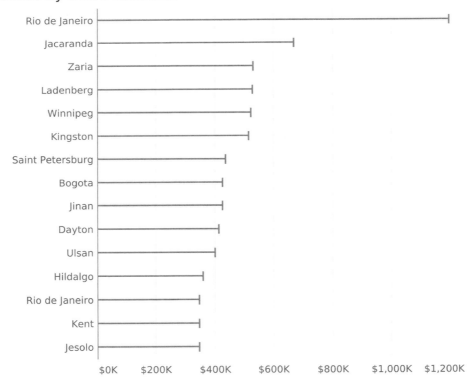

FIGURE 4.5 Thin bar chart with vertical lines.

Bar Chart with Average Reference Line

Suppose we wanted to see which stores were above and below average, and by how much? Figure 4.6 is an example of a bar chart with a reference line.

Here we can see that six stores are above average and the rest are below. We can also see *how much* above or below average they are because the average line provides a common baseline from which we can estimate position.

Sales by Store Location

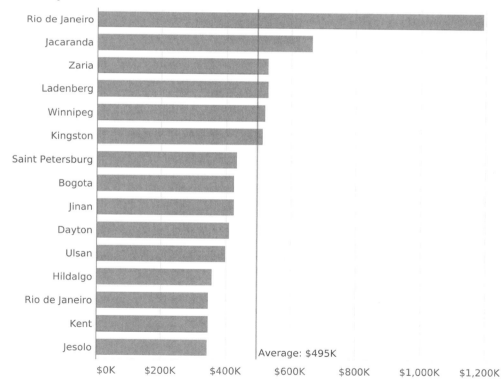

FIGURE 4.6 Bar chart with reference line.

Bar Chart with a Goal Reference Line

Suppose we want to know which stores performed above and below their individual goals,

and by how much? We could have a reference line for each bar (Figure 4.7).

Maybe we want to make it easier to see which stores are below goal? We can do that by sorting and grouping (Figure 4.8).

Sales by Store Location (| = Goal)

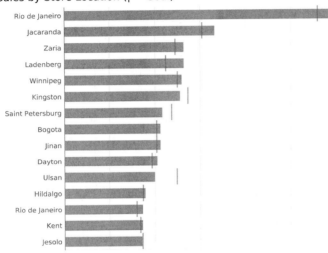

FIGURE 4.7 Bar chart with reference lines, making it easy to see which stores are above or below goal, and by how much.

Sales by Store Location (| = Goal)

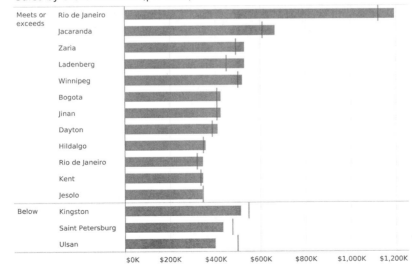

FIGURE 4.8 Grouping and sorting to segregate stores that meet or exceed their goals from those that do not.

We can also color code the bars (Figure 4.9).

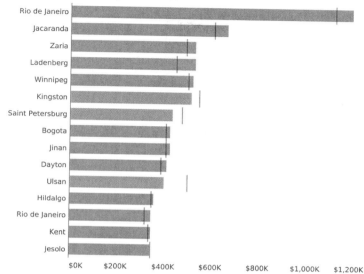

FIGURE 4.9 Bar chart with reference lines and underperforming stores highlighted in orange.

The Power of the Little Dot

Here's another technique that is remarkably useful to help people notice important information: the little red dot (Figure 4.10)!

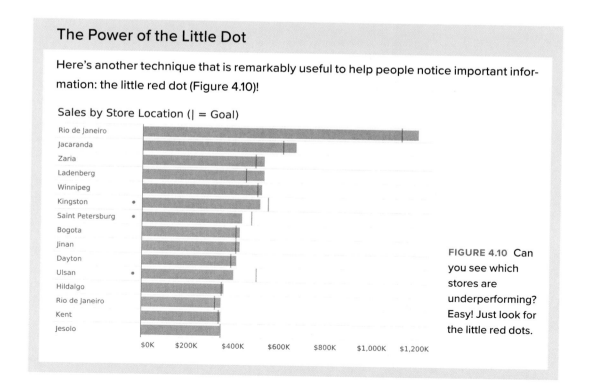

FIGURE 4.10 Can you see which stores are underperforming? Easy! Just look for the little red dots.

The Paired or Clustered Bar Chart and Alternatives

How do you compare data for two or more segments across multiple categories? For example, maybe you want to compare sales for three product categories across five different countries. How do you show this?

The go-to approach is the clustered bar chart, but this type of chart can be dense and confusing if you have lots of categories, so you should be aware of some good alternatives.

Let's start first with the simple paired bar chart and see how it works.

Paired Bar Chart

The paired bar chart is a very popular way to compare a single measure for two segments (in this case profit for 2019 and 2018) across multiple categories (Figure 4.11).

This approach is solid analytically because we show length/position from a common baseline; however, the chart is very dense and will become very cluttered if we were to show more than two years of data. What are some possible alternatives?

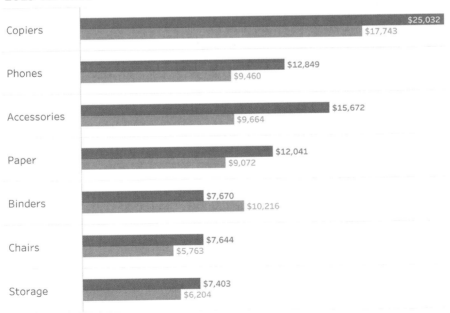

Profit Comparison
2019 vs. 2018

Copiers	$25,032 / $17,743
Phones	$12,849 / $9,460
Accessories	$15,672 / $9,664
Paper	$12,041 / $9,072
Binders	$7,670 / $10,216
Chairs	$7,644 / $5,763
Storage	$7,403 / $6,204

FIGURE 4.11 A paired bar chart showing sales for 2019 and 2018 across multiple categories.

Bar Chart with Reference Line

The reference line we used earlier to compare actuals against a goal also works well to compare the profit for two different years. Figure 4.12 shows a bar chart with a reference line where the bars represent profit for 2019 and the vertical lines represent profit for 2018.

Notice that this enables us to gauge the magnitude of profit for the different categories in 2019 and see which categories' profits were more (or less) than the previous year, and by how much.

Another advantage is that this takes up much less space than the paired bar chart (Figure 4.11). That said, we will run into problems if we try to compare more than two periods as we'll need either another bar, another line, or some other symbol.

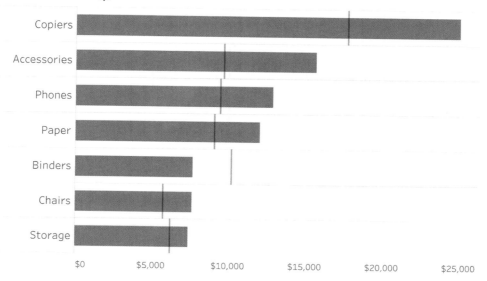

Profit Comparison
2019 vs. 2018 (|)

FIGURE 4.12 A bar chart with a reference line is a great way to compare one period (the bars) with a previous period (the vertical lines).

Bar-in-Bar Chart

Another approach that works well is a bar-in-bar chart (Figure 4.13).

It shares the same pros and cons as the bar chart with a reference line: it is more compact than the paired bar chart, but would not be able to display more than two years of data well. For three years, we'd need a bar-in-bar-in-bar chart, and that could get unwieldy.

Horizontal Gap Charts

Let's take a very brief break from this profit data set and consider the question: how do organizations that are really good at visualizing data show this type of thing? One of my favorites is the Pew Research Center. How might they show the gaps between different years or segments? Consider the example in Figure 4.14, which shows the difference in opinion among Black, Hispanic, and White survey respondents to a survey Pew Research Center conducted in late 2018.

I've labeled this a gap chart, but there are a lot of names for this chart type (connected dot plot, dumbbell chart, and barbell chart). Gap charts do a very good job of showing the differences across three different segments (in this case Black, Hispanic, and White respondents) across multiple measures. Here's how this approach would work for our profit data (Figure 4.15).

This type of chart is very versatile. Not only is it very compact, but it can also show more

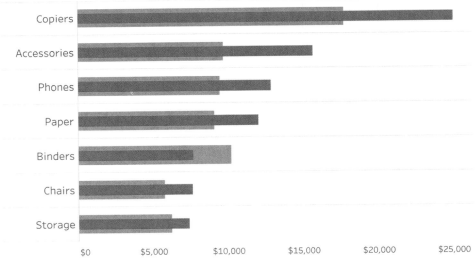

Profit Comparison
2019 vs. 2018

FIGURE 4.13 A bar-in-bar chart allows us to compare the current period (green) with the previous period (gray).

Black Americans and Hispanics are more concerned about police officers' efforts

% of U.S. adults who say police officers _____ all or most, or some of the time

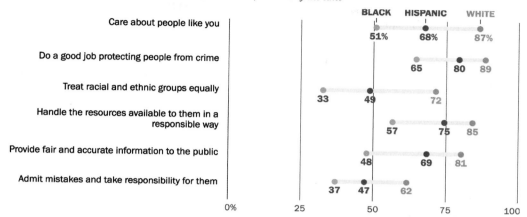

Source: Survey conducted Nov. 27-Dec. 10, 2018, among U.S. adults.
"Why Americans Don't Fully Trust Many Who Hold Positions of Power and Responsibility"

FIGURE 4.14   A Pew Research Center gap chart (Pew Research Center).

Profit Comparison
2019 vs. 2018

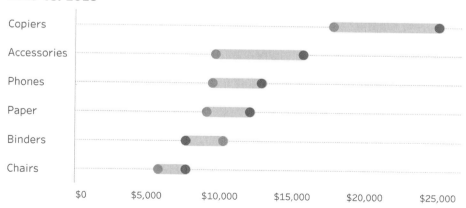

FIGURE 4.15   A connected dot plot shows the difference between 2019 and 2018 profits across multiple categories.

than two segments. That said, if you have four or more segments (e.g., four years of data), this chart, like the clustered bar chart, can become difficult to read. We'll explore how to address this in Chapter 7.

Comet Chart

While I think the gap chart is the most versatile, the comet chart (Figure 4.16) has become my go-to when showing the change between two periods, or in any type of situation where there is ordinal data (e.g., older to newer, junior to senior, etc.).

It's very easy to see which categories had an upswing, which had a downswing, and by how much. (The Binders category immediately stands out, which was not the case in Figure 4.15.) This chart would also allow me to add a reference for each category to specify a goal. This means I could easily compare this year to last year and see if we are ahead of or behind our goals (and by how much) for this year.

I love the comet chart, but I've got colleagues who think both the tadpole or the arrow chart work as well, if not better (Figure 4.17).

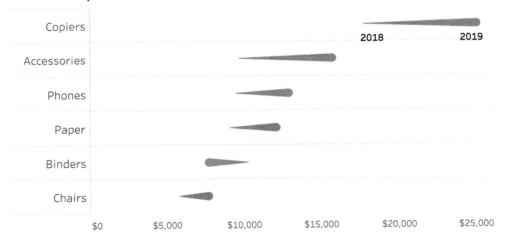

Profit Comparison

FIGURE 4.16 A comet chart where the head is 2019 and the tail is 2018.

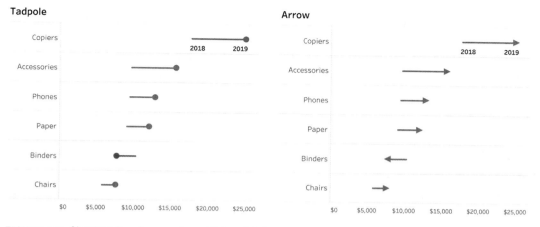

FIGURE 4.17 Showing the changes from 2018 to 2019 using a tadpole and an arrow chart.

An Introduction to the Slopegraph

I'll discuss this chart in more detail in the section on timelines, but I would be remiss if I did not show the slopegraph because it is a great way to present the change in profit over two years (Figure 4.18).

Like the other charts in this section, it shows the position from a common baseline to allow people to make easy and accurate comparisons.

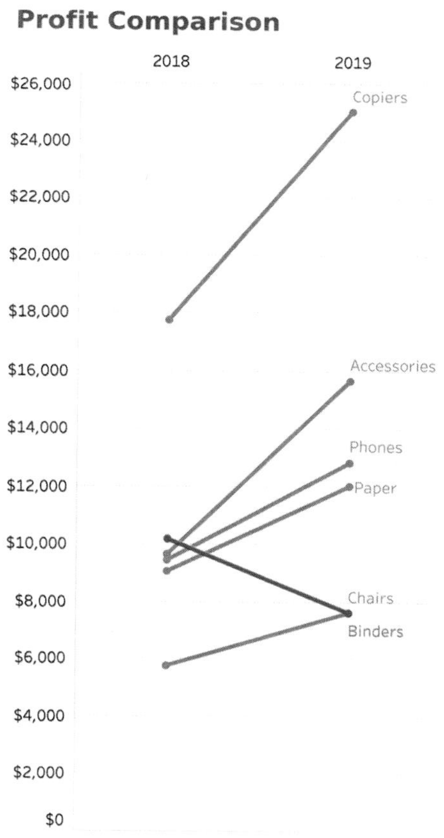

Profit Comparison

FIGURE 4.18 A slopegraph showing the change in profit for different categories between 2018 and 2019.

Scatterplots

You may have no trouble understanding bar charts, stacked bars, pie charts, and so on, but maybe you are less comfortable with scatterplots.* Or maybe you understand them, but you have colleagues who aren't sure why they would be useful. Let's look at some examples that will help you show how they work and why they can be so valuable.

Example 1: Ice Cream Parlor

Let's say you manage an ice cream parlor. There are probably a lot of different factors you track, including number of customers, sales of cups versus cones, inventory, weather's effect on sales, and so on. Suppose you were curious to see if there was a relationship between outside temperature and how much ice cream you sell; specifically, do you sell more on warm days? If so, how much more?

You have a year of data at your disposal, and you decide to start by looking at just three days' worth (Figure 4.19.).

Looking at the bottom dot, we can see that the high temperature was quite cold on February 8 (35 degrees Fahrenheit), and we sold

FIGURE 4.19 A simple scatterplot that shows the relationship between temperature (along the bottom, on the x-axis) and ice cream sold (along the left side, on the y-axis).

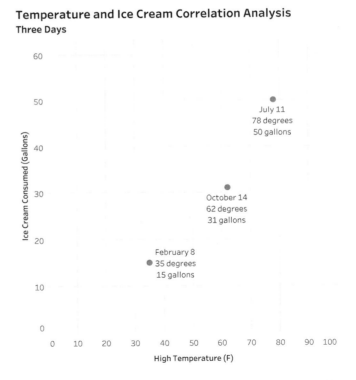

Temperature and Ice Cream Correlation Analysis
Three Days

only 15 gallons of ice cream. Compare that with the top dot for July 11 when the high temperature was 78 degrees, and we sold 50 gallons of ice cream.

It looks like there may be something to our theory, but three data points is not enough to draw a meaningful conclusion. Let's see what this looks like when we plot 365 days' worth of data (Figure 4.20).

In this scatterplot each dot represents a different day. With the exception of that one dot that's all by itself, can you see that dots that are toward the right are also toward the top, and those toward the left are closer to the bottom?

Temperature and Ice Cream Correlation Analysis
365 Days

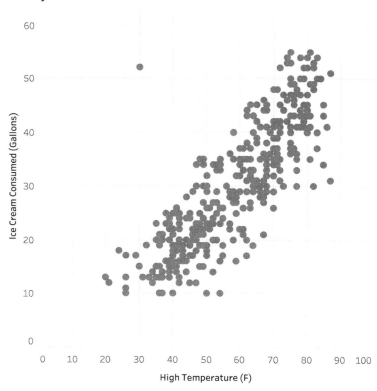

FIGURE 4.20 Plotting temperature versus ice cream eaten for a full year. There are 365 dots on this scatterplot, each dot representing a different day.

Statisticians often want to see if there is a clear linear relationship between two measures and will calculate and plot a linear regression line (Figure 4.21).

I won't get into the particulars of what the statistical values mean, except to say that this is a pretty good model to be able to predict the *dependent* value (the amount of ice cream eaten) based on the *independent* value (the temperature outside). It is the convention to always place the independent variable on the x-axis and the dependent variable on the y-axis. In this case determining which is which is pretty easy because consuming ice cream won't change the temperature outside, but the temperature outside clearly has an impact on the amount of ice cream consumed.

If you're curious about that outlier, here is a triple-encoded version of the chart that includes an annotation that explains the lonely dot (Figure 4.22).

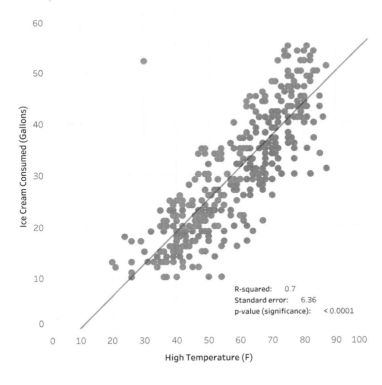

Temperature and Ice Cream Correlation Analysis
365 Days with Trend Line

R-squared: 0.7
Standard error: 6.36
p-value (significance):   < 0.0001

FIGURE 4.21 Scatterplot with linear trend line. The line is there to help predict the amount of ice cream consumed according to the temperature.

Temperature and Ice Cream Correlation Analysis

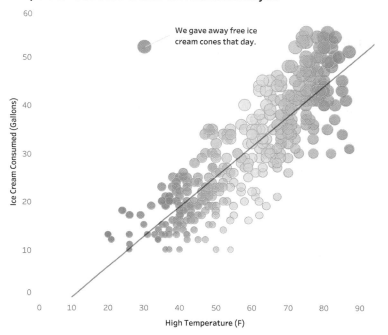

We gave away free ice cream cones that day.

FIGURE 4.22 Fully-rendered scatterplot with additional encoding showing the relationship between temperature and amount of ice cream sold.

Yes, but Where Are My Numbers?

At this point you and your colleagues may be wondering, "What's up with this? Suppose I want to know how much ice cream was consumed on a particular day? How can I get that from this chart?"

This view, a scatterplot by itself, won't answer that question, but a dashboard that combines several different charts can answer that question and show the relationship between outside temperature and ice cream consumption. We'll explore dashboards in Chapter 7.

OK, so now we understand why, even though it was cold, we sold a lot of ice cream that one day: we were literally giving it away! As for the term *triple encoded*, it refers to adding some elements that we don't need to decipher the graph. The primary encoding is position because a dot further to the right means the weather was hotter and one further up means we sold more ice cream. But we're adding two more ways to encode the data: color (orange for hot and blue for cold) and size (a large dot means more ice cream and a small dot means less ice cream).

To be clear, the most important element in this scatterplot is position from a common baseline. Color and size just help amplify the findings.

What's Up with That Annotation on the Outlier in the Ice Cream Example?

While it is possible to program a smart dashboard that automatically annotates outliers, in this case, I, and not the coding, chose to annotate something I thought was important. This is an instance of using a dashboard to find something interesting and then presenting that curated finding to others. We'll explore this further in Chapter 7.

Example 2: Salary Distribution

Let's leave the ice cream parlor behind. In this second example, we'll look at a data set of the salaries of 400 employees in an organization, with each dot representing an employee (Figure 4.23).

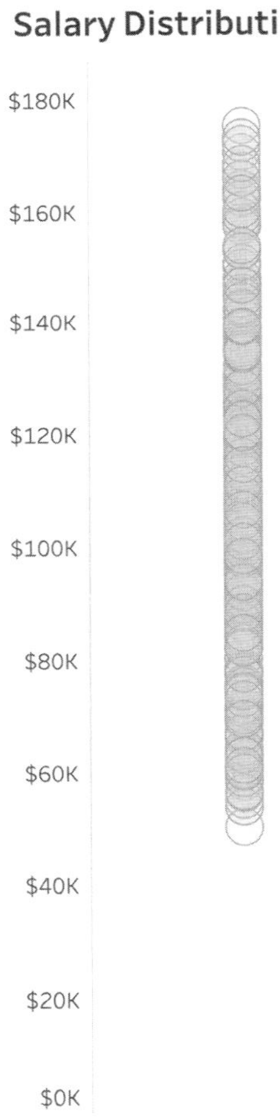

FIGURE 4.23 Employee salaries presented in a strip plot.

If you're thinking, "What good is this? There's just a bunch of dots, and I can't tell where there's a high concentration," then you are not alone. That is why statisticians and scientists will often overlay a box and whisker plot (Figure 4.24).

The box portion shows quartiles. The point where the boxes connect is the median (fiftieth percentile), the upper part of the box is the seventy-fifth percentile, and the lower portion is the twenty-fifth percentile. The whisker at each end represents a demarcation point; any dots beyond them are considered *outliers.**

Salary Distribution

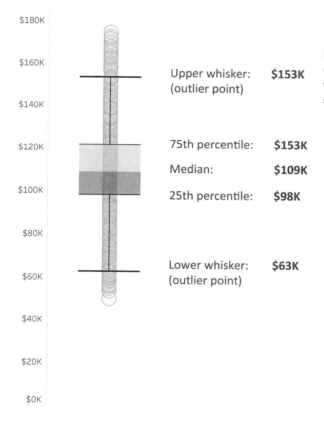

Upper whisker: $153K
(outlier point)

75th percentile: $153K

Median: $109K

25th percentile: $98K

Lower whisker: $63K
(outlier point)

FIGURE 4.24 Salary for each employee as a strip plot with a box and whisker plot superimposed.

---

* What constitutes an outlier? The person who added the whiskers to the box plot was John Tukey, and he defined it as 1.5 times the interquartile range (1.5 times the difference between the twenty-fifth percentile and seventy-fifth percentile). The box and whisker plot is also called a Tukey plot, but bragging rights to the box plot belong to Mary Eleanor Spear who first proposed the idea of "range bars" in 1952. Maybe we should call it a Spear plot? See https://medium.com/nightingale/credit-where-credit-is-due-mary-eleanor-spear-6a7a1951b8e6.

I'm not a fan of box and whisker plots, and most of my audience does not understand how to read them. I prefer showing the distribution using lines and shaded areas (Figure 4.25).

Actually, my first choice would be to show this distribution as a jitterplot.

Jitterplots

Our salary data contains 400 dots, and it's hard to see all of them in a strip plot because so many are on top of each other. To show this data another way, we can randomly jitter the dots left and right to get a sense of how many dots there are and where they are concentrated (Figure 4.26).

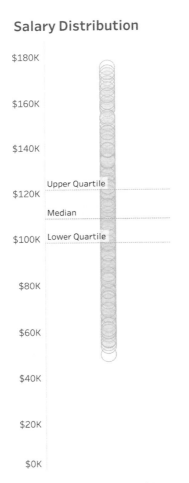

FIGURE 4.25 A strip plot with lines and shaded areas showing quartiles.

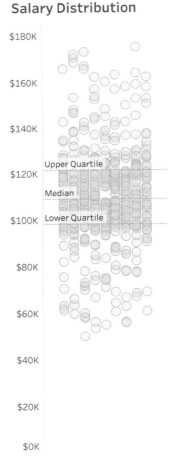

FIGURE 4.26 Salary data presented as a jitterplot.

I'll admit that upon first seeing this, some people wonder if there's any difference between a dot that's toward the left and one that's toward the right. I need to explain that all I've done is take the dots that were in a single vertical strip and moved some of them to the left and some to the right so we can see all the dots. In short, it makes no difference how far left or right a dot lands.

Is seeing the disaggregated data worth the trouble? Again, why not just show summary statistics?

Consider an interactive system in which a person can log in and see her/his performance compared to peers with respect to sales, bugs fixed, support tickets closed, or other metrics.

Let's look at a salary dashboard where you can see how much you are being paid compared with others in the same industry, job level, and so on. Consider Figure 4.27, where you can see your salary versus the average salary of all your peers.

Salary Distribution
You compared with everybody else

FIGURE 4.27 Comparing an individual's salary with the average of all others.

When I show this to workshop attendees, I ask them how angry this makes them. Most say they aren't really angry as they imagine they may not have as many years of experience or haven't been with the company as long as others in a similar position. I then show them the exact same information, but with disaggregated data (Figure 4.28).

This is a major eye opener. How would you ever see this with just a spreadsheet? We're looking at the same information (your salary of $89,349), and we see exactly where you stand with respect to others in the disaggregated example. This reminds me of one of my favorite illustrations from Ben Orlin's book *Math with Bad Drawings* (Figure 4.29).

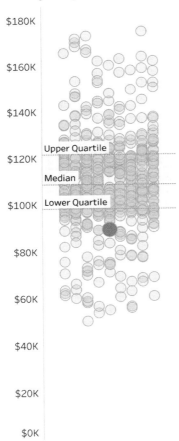

FIGURE 4.28 The same individual compared with everyone else using disaggregated data.

FIGURE 4.29 The problems with summary statistics (in this case, the arithmetic mean or average), as illustrated by Ben Orlin (Illustration by Ben Orlin from *Math with Bad Drawings: Illuminating the Ideas that Shape Our Reality* by Ben Orlin).

In Figure 4.30 we see another way to present an individual's salary compared with others' using a Wilkinson dot plot (also called a unit histogram).

Many of my clients prefer this approach to the jitterplot because they get a better sense of how the measure (in this case, salary) is distributed.

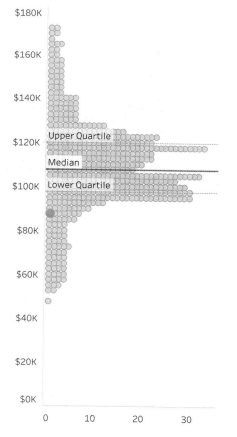

Salary Distribution
You compared with everybody else

What Happens if There Are Many More Dots?

I admit that this approach ("here's what interests you, and here it is with respect to everyone else") doesn't scale if you have thousands, let alone, millions of dots. Fans of Douglas Adams's *The Hitchhiker's Guide to the Galaxy* may recall the Total Perspective Vortex. It was a torture device designed to show how insignificant an individual is with respect to the vastness of all time and space. Putting the torture aside, one way to address this problem of scale is first to compare a group you are in with other groups, and then show where you are within your respective group.

I like both the jitterplot and the Wilkinson dot plot and, depending on the situation, would work with my stakeholders to decide which one better serves the intended audience.

We'll look into the power of comparing an individual data point with a larger data set in Chapter 5.

FIGURE 4.30 Salary data presented using a Wilkinson dot plot.

Stacked Bar Charts and Area Charts

When used properly, stacked bar charts and area charts can be great to show both an overall comparison as well as a part-to-whole comparison, but it's important to be careful with them.

Consider the image shown in Figure 4.31, where visualization designer Matt Chambers compares the number of punches thrown in the

Floyd Mayweather Jr.–Conor McGregor heavyweight prizefight in 2017.

Goodness, McGregor threw so many more punches. He must have won.

Now let's see what happens if instead of just showing the total punches thrown, we also compare the punches that landed (Figure 4.32).

Now, it's very easy for me to make the comparisons and get a good idea of why Mayweather

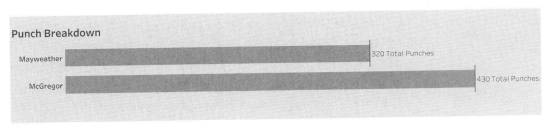

FIGURE 4.31 A comparison of overall punches thrown in a 2017 heavyweight prize fight (Matt Chambers).

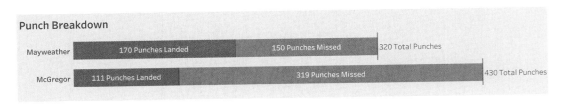

FIGURE 4.32 Punches landed versus punches thrown (Matt Chambers).

won the fight. Look at how many more punches McGregor threw than Mayweather (430 versus 320). That must have been exhausting for McGregor. And look at how many more of Mayweather's punches actually landed (170 versus 111). You can also see that Mayweather landed more than half of his punches, while McGregor landed only about one-quarter. I think this is a great stacked bar chart.

Where Stacked Bar Charts Fail

You may recall my earlier discussion about trying to compare the length of floating bars (see Chapter 2, Figure 2.14). I mentioned that chart designers inadvertently ask you to make difficult comparisons when they present their audience with stacked bar charts that have more than two categories.

Consider the dashboard shown in Figure 4.33.

Sales by Region Dashboard

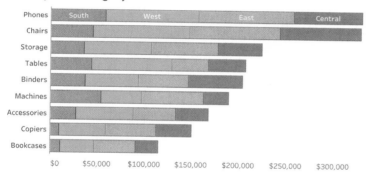

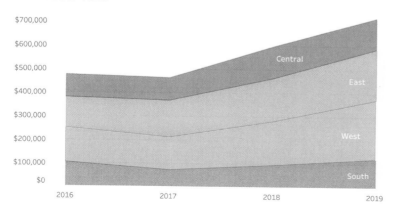

FIGURE 4.33 A sales dashboard with a stacked bar chart and an area chart.

I often see stacked bar charts (and their cousin, the stacked area chart) in marketing materials for many of the major data visualization tool vendors. Maybe it's because they look cool, but cool and useful are two different things. We need to remember that we want to play into what people do well (comparing bar length from a common baseline) and avoid what they're not good at, (comparing those inner bars).

Here's the problem: try to compare the length of segments that aren't hugging the baseline (Figure 4.34). For example, are sales for Storage in the East bigger or smaller than Machines in the East (the third and sixth bars)? What about sales for Binders versus Copiers (the fifth and eighth bars)?

There are elements of this stacked bar chart that are useful; for example, it's easy to compare the *overall* sales, as we see in Figure 4.35.

Sales by Sub-category

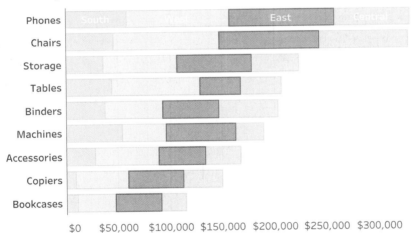

FIGURE 4.34 It's difficult to compare the lengths of bars that don't have a common baseline.

Sales by Sub-category

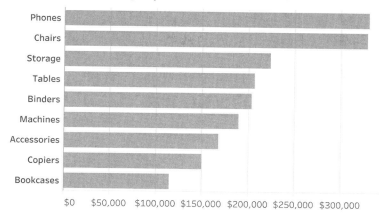

FIGURE 4.35 Comparing the overall sales; we're not taking region into account.

Highlighting the South region is also useful because we can easily make comparisons across the sub-categories and gauge the part-to-whole ratio within a category (Figure 4.36).

It's easy to see that the sales for the South region for Phones (the top red bar) is about the same as the sales in the South for Machines (the sixth red bar). We can also see that the South region doesn't account for much of the sales across any of the sub-categories with the exception of Machines, where it accounts for about one-quarter of total sales.

Sales by Sub-category

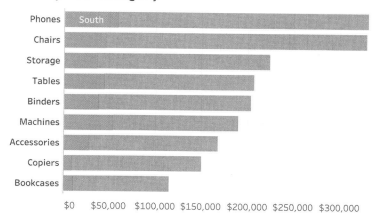

FIGURE 4.36 Highlighting one region (the one along the baseline) and comparing it with the sub-category's overall sales.

Note that we are sorting the sub-categories from overall highest to overall lowest. Since we are focusing on the South, maybe it would be easier to understand the data if we sorted from highest to lowest within that region (Figure 4.37).

Sales by Sub-category

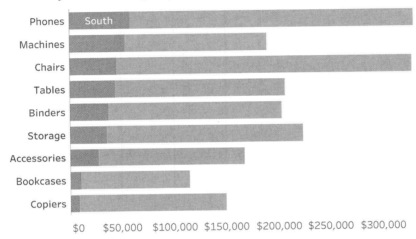

FIGURE 4.37 Sorting from highest to lowest based on sales in the South region. An interactive dashboard would allow you to sort the bars.

How Do We "Un-scaredy-cat-ify" the Main Visualization?

These last few visualizations have been very useful in showing that we can compare whatever category is hugging the baseline as well as the overall sales. Is there a way to change what is at the baseline and compare that? Yes! Many modern data visualization tools allow the audience to change the featured region (Figure 4.38). This is a *huge* argument for offering your audience interactivity (more in Chapter 7).

By allowing your audience to focus on the overall sales and one region at a time, we can turn a "scaredy-cat" into a truly useful visualization.

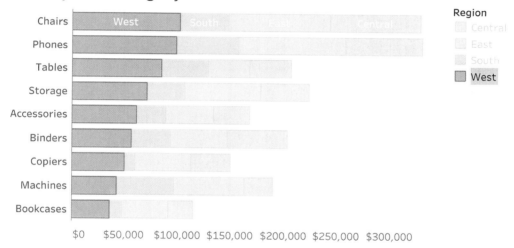

FIGURE 4.38 A dashboard that makes it easy to focus on any region. Here the West is selected.

Understanding Area Charts

What is an area chart? It's a version of a stacked bar chart in which you show measures over time and connect time periods, much like a line chart. Let's start with a stacked bar chart and turn it into an area chart.

Figure 4.39 shows how we might track sales over time by region, using a bar chart.

Figure 4.40 shows the same data as an area chart.

The area chart suffers from the same problem as stacked bar charts: you can easily compare the overall amounts and whatever is along the baseline, but you can't compare any of the other segments. There's an interesting fact about the Central region that is not apparent, unless it's shown along the baseline (Figure 4.41).

Central is the only region that saw a *decrease* between 2018 and 2019, but we can only discern that easily if Central is displayed along the baseline.

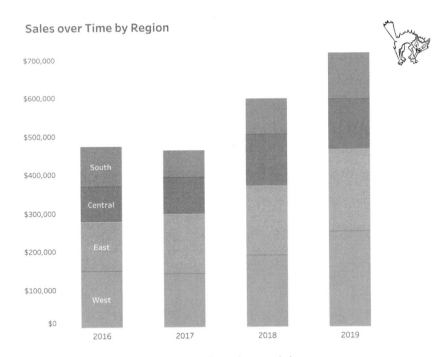

Sales over Time by Region

FIGURE 4.39 Stacked bar chart showing sales trends by year.

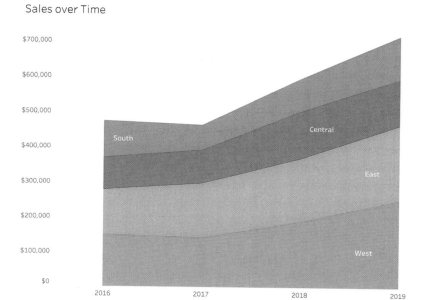

FIGURE 4.40 Area chart showing sales by region over time.

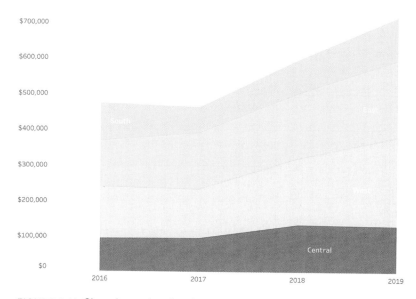

FIGURE 4.41 Changing order of regions reveals something interesting about the Central region.

Line Charts and Other Ways to Visualize Time

The line chart is the go-to chart for showing trends over time. Consider the example in Figure 4.42, where we see sales trends over a 12-month period.

If you are like me, you can see that, for the most part, sales appear to be increasing, with the exception of February and November when there were dips.

Why a line chart? We could certainly use a bar chart (Figure 4.43), but I don't think it is as easy to see the dips, plus the continuous nature of the dates is lost. The line shows the flow of one month into the next. This is probably why, going back to the eighteenth century, the world settled on this type of chart to show trends over time.*

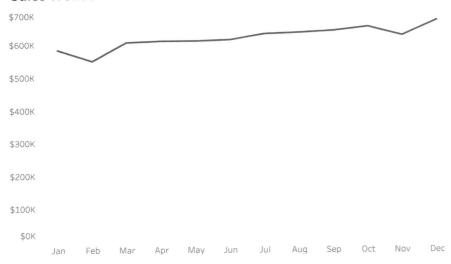

Sales Trends

FIGURE 4.42 A line chart showing sales trends over a 12-month period.

---

* In 1753 Jacques Barbeau-Duborg published his *Chronographie Universelle*, a 54-foot-long chart mounted on an apparatus with cranks that allow the reader to scroll through the history of the world as shown by the births and deaths of every famous person going back to the beginning of creation (thought to be about 4,000 years earlier) through the present day. Many historians consider this ground zero for the regularly spaced x-axis to depict time. A copy of the *Chronographie* on its scrolling apparatus is part of the Princeton University Library rare book collection. Barbeau-Duborg came up with the idea of presenting the data going left to right in equal increments. It was William Playfair who expanded on this in 1786 and published the first line graphs in his *The Commercial and Political Atlas*. I got to see and touch both of these works, along with Joseph Priestly's *Chart of History* and *Chart of Biography* in 2019 when I visited Princeton with two of my friends and colleagues, Andy Cotreave and RJ Andrews. Andy wrote about our bucket list visit at BigPic.me/timelines.

The bar chart does have one big advantage over the line chart: we can flip it 90 degrees and still read it. Look what happens when we flip the line chart by 90 degrees (Figure 4.44).

Yikes! The chart that was so easy to read when oriented left to right is very difficult to interpret when it goes from top down. Why is that?

People in most cultures, even those that read from right to left or from top down, have learned to look at time as going from left to

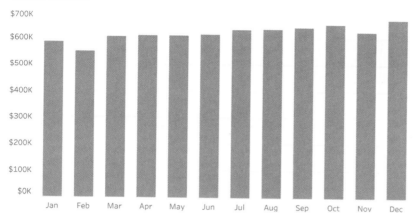

Sales Trends

FIGURE 4.43 A bar chart showing the same sales trends.

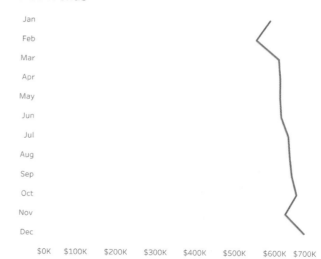

Sales Trends

FIGURE 4.44 Timeline flipped 90 degrees.

right in equally spaced increments, with dinosaurs all the way to the left and Star Trek a bit to the right. That said, I encourage you to get used to seeing the timeline on its side, as mobile devices and scrolling are already starting to shift how people view time (Figure 4.45).

I also want people to be familiar with ways of visualizing time that don't simply go from

oldest to newest, as there are insights you will miss if you look at time only chronologically.

Consider sales data showing trends over a four-year period (Figure 4.46).

Suppose you wanted to know in which months sales were particularly good. Let's see what happens if we look at the same four-year period but show monthly data (Figure 4.47).

Can you tell in which months sales were good? Not month and year, but over the four-year period, are there particular months that

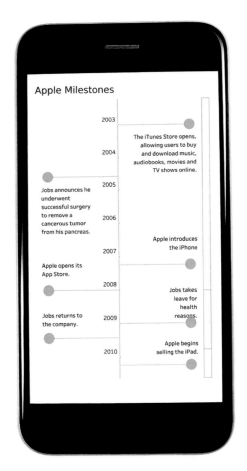

FIGURE 4.45 A vertical timeline with a scroll bar displayed on a mobile phone.

FIGURE 4.46 Sales by year, 2016–2019.

are good and those that are bad? If you can answer this question, you have skills few people have, as it's hard to group the same months together because they are separated by different years. Suppose, instead, we combined the results for each month (e.g., all the January results, February results, etc.), and show the totals by month for all four years (Figure 4.48)?

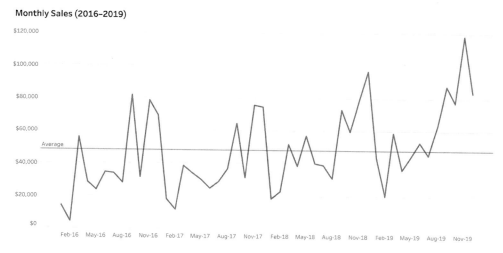

Monthly Sales (2016–2019)

FIGURE 4.47 Sales by month over a four-year period.

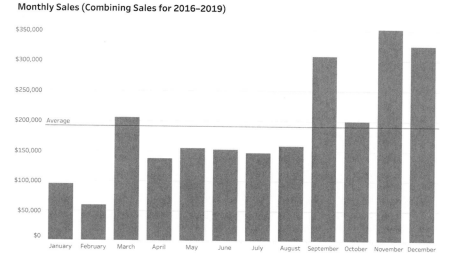

Monthly Sales (Combining Sales for 2016–2019)

FIGURE 4.48 Group sales for all four years into each month to see which months have the best sales.

Now the question is very easy to answer: November is the best month and February is the worst month. But was that always the case? Maybe there was just one year in which November had amazing sales. We can determine this by taking the same number of data points as we had in the noisy chart in Figure 4.47 and changing the order of how we group things. That is, instead of starting with year and breaking it down by each month, we start with the month and break it down for each year, as in Figure 4.49.

November was always a good month for sales, but particularly in 2019. This is much easier to understand than the traditional approach to displaying dates (year then month, going from old to new).

You may use the same technique to see on which day of the week you have the greatest sales. Figure 4.50 shows the same data, broken down by year and then day.

Yes, it it's easy to see when we had some terrific sales, but it's impossible to determine on which day of the week, overall, sales are good or bad. Contrast that with the approach in Figure 4.51, which shows sales by day of the week and year.

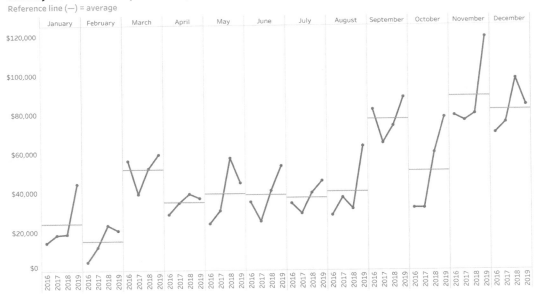

Sales by Month and Year (2016–2019)
Reference line (—) = average

FIGURE 4.49 Sales by month, broken down by year.

Daily Sales (2016–2019)

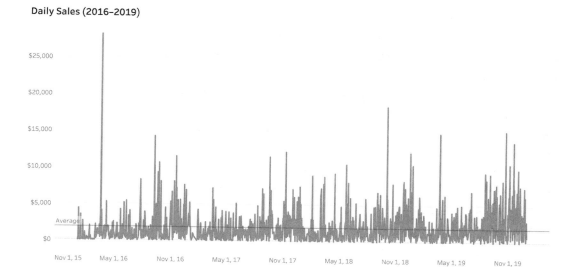

FIGURE 4.50 Sales by day over a four-year period. Unless you have an a very fine eye for this, there's little signal and lots of noise.

Sales by Day of the Week and Year (2016–2019)

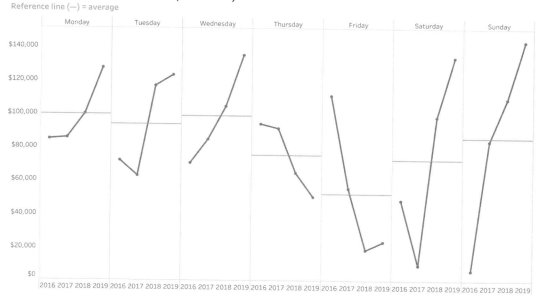

FIGURE 4.51 Sales by day of the week broken down by year.

Look at how many questions this chart answers. Better than that, look at how many questions it poses (e.g., Why did sales drop so much on Thursday and Friday? Why the huge increase in sales the past two years for Saturday and Sunday?) You can't see *any* of that with the more traditional approach (Figure 4.50).

Index Charts

"How are we doing this quarter compared to last quarter and compared to a year ago this quarter?" Goodness, if I had an actual quarter for every time this type of analysis has come up in my career. This seems like an easy question, but maybe we're only halfway into the current quarter. How do you compare something that is only half-finished with something that happened previously and is completed? Consider the typical timeline view in Figure 4.52.

There's a really big spike early in the most recent quarter, but we want to know cumulative sales, so instead of showing sales per day let's try a running sum of sales for the quarter (Figure 4.53).

We can see that sales for the previous quarter weren't that good, but it's still hard to compare the different quarters because they're spaced out by older dates to newer dates. Suppose, instead, we aligned them all to start at the same point: the first week in any given quarter. We can do this using an index chart (Figure 4.54).

Instead of dates along the x-axis, we see week numbers. Here we're comparing 22 quarters of data. Note that there were no sales on Week 1 of the previous quarter. And we can see that even though we're only 10 weeks into the current quarter, it is on track to be one of the best quarters ever.

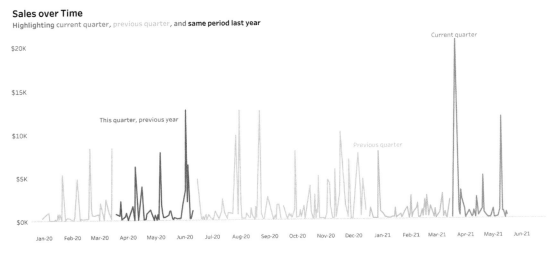

FIGURE 4.52 Line chart showing sales by date over a two-year period, highlighting selected quarters.

Sales over Time
Highlighting current quarter, previous quarter, and **same period last year**

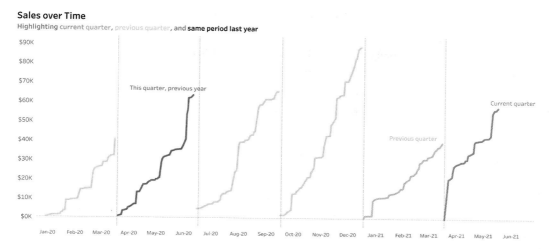

FIGURE 4.53 A line chart showing cumulative sales by date over a two-year period and highlighting selected quarters.

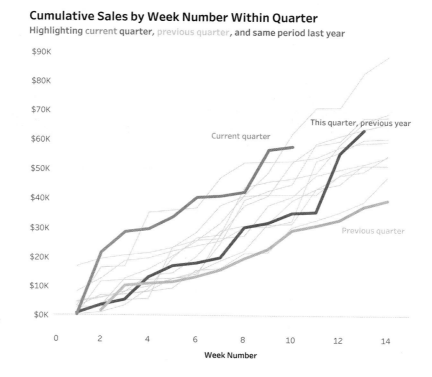

FIGURE 4.54 An index chart allows us to compare events that started at different times by imagining they all started at the same point.

Curious about that other quarter when sales were really good (the one tracking similarly to the current quarter)? Maybe we could also highlight the best quarter and worst quarter? Or perhaps, on an interactive dashboard, we could let our audience explore this on their own. (We'll discuss this in detail in Chapter 7.)

The index chart went mainstream during the coronavirus pandemic as people needed to be able to compare how their country (or state or city) was faring compared to other locales. In Figure 4.55 we see an index chart from the *Financial Times* that allows us to compare Covid-19 cases in different countries, even though the pandemic broke out at different times during the year.

The line for China is longer than all the other lines because the first cases were recorded

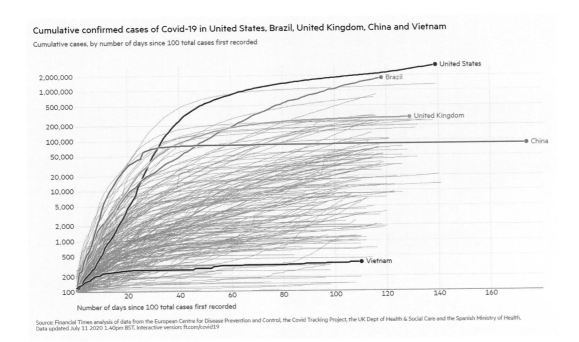

Cumulative confirmed cases of Covid-19 in United States, Brazil, United Kingdom, China and Vietnam

Cumulative cases, by number of days since 100 total cases first recorded

Number of days since 100 total cases first recorded

Source: Financial Times analysis of data from the European Centre for Disease Prevention and Control, the Covid Tracking Project, the UK Dept of Health & Social Care and the Spanish Ministry of Health. Data updated July 11 2020 1.40pm BST. Interactive version: ft.com/covid19

FIGURE 4.55 A *Financial Times* index chart comparing cumulative confirmed cases of Covid-19 from a common starting point of days since 100 total cases were first recorded, as of July 11, 2020. (*Financial Times* / FT.com, July 11, 2020. Used under license from the *Financial Times*. All rights reserved. See BigPic.me /ftcharts for an interactive version.)

there weeks before Covid-19 appeared in other countries. If you look carefully, you will also notice that the y-axis is using a logarithmic scale and not a linear scale. This logarithmic scale increases in powers of 10. If you are curious about why these jumps are so useful for this data, see the video at BigPic.me/logscales.

Let's Take a Break and Let You Try

Armed with what you've seen so far, let's see how you would do visualizing a simple data set.

Consider the data in Figure 4.56, which shows the market share for Pizza Hut and Domino's over a 10-year period.

I encourage you to take a piece of paper and two different colored pens, and try to come up with a way to display the data. Don't worry about making it accurate or neatly drawn. Just take a stab at something that would help you and others see and understand the data.

Market Share over Time

Year	Domino's	Pizza Hut
2007	27%	44%
2008	25%	45%
2009	26%	41%
2010	26%	42%
2011	26%	43%
2012	24%	41%
2013	25%	39%
2014	26%	35%
2015	28%	33%
2016	30%	31%

FIGURE 4.56   A text table showing market share over time.

There are many different ways you can present this data clearly. Let's look at some of them, including how the *Wall Street Journal* presented it in an article, a facsimile of which is shown in Figure 4.57.

I remember when I saw this, I thought, "Why these colors?" and "Would I have presented the data differently?" You may recall that I'm not a big fan of the paired bar chart because it takes up a lot of room and is dense, but it is analytically sound, so I have no quarrel if this is how you would want to present it. By the way, I don't have an answer about the colors, as they don't appear to be in the official color palette of either company.

Let's look at some different approaches that workshop attendees have developed for this data.

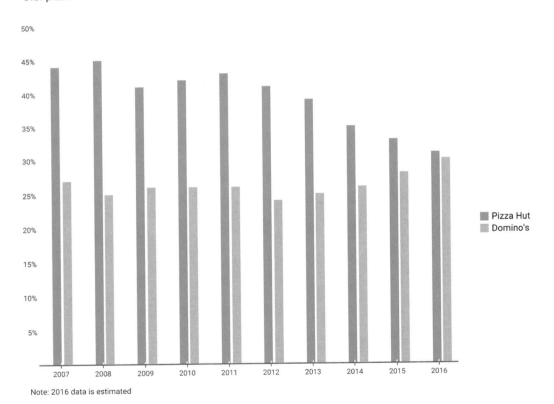

Bigger Slice
U.S. pizza chain market shares

Note: 2016 data is estimated

FIGURE 4.57 A paired bar chart showing market share over time (data from Restaurant Research via Hedgeye).

Bar-in-Bar Charts

Figure 4.58 shows the data rendered using a bar-in-bar chart.

The pushback I've gotten from clients and colleagues is that we're giving more heft to the wider bar and may be tipping the scales unfairly toward Pizza Hut. The bars aren't just taller; they are also wider.

Vertical Gap Chart

Figure 4.59 presents the same data rendered using a gap chart, which you'll remember can also be called a connected dot plot or a barbell chart.

Line Chart

Figure 4.60 shows the same data rendered as a line chart.

Bigger Slice
U.S. pizza chain market shares
Pizza Hut | Domino's

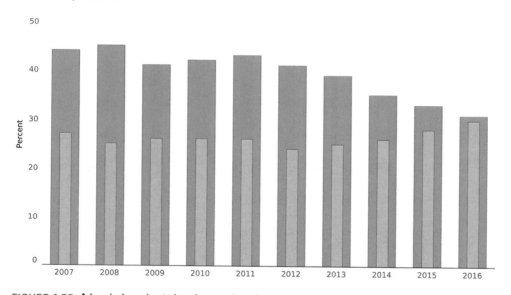

FIGURE 4.58 A bar-in-bar chart showing market share over time (data from Restaurant Research via Hedgeye).

Bigger Slice
U.S. pizza chain market shares

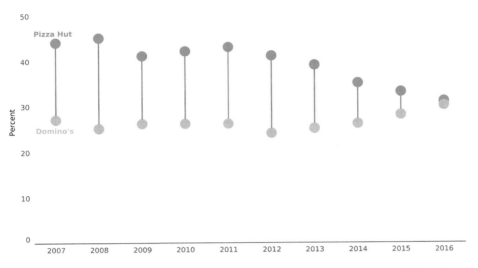

FIGURE 4.59 A gap chart showing market share over time (data from Restaurant Research via Hedgeye).

Bigger Slice
U.S. pizza chain market shares

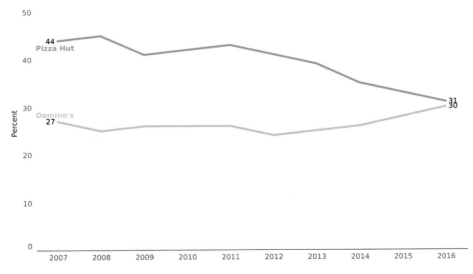

FIGURE 4.60 A line chart showing market share over time (data from Restaurant Research via Hedgeye).

Line Chart with Shading

Figure 4.61 presents the same data rendered as a line chart/area chart hybrid where the gap between the two lines is shaded.*

Divergent Bar Chart

Figure 4.62 shows another way to render the data that I *don't* think is OK. There's nothing inherently wrong with a divergent stacked bar chart (they are particularly useful for survey data), but here it only allows me to compare the brand against itself because there's no common baseline for both Pizza Hut and Domino's. That is, I can see that 2008 was the best year for Pizza Hut and 2016 was the best year for Domino's, but I can't compare values for Pizza Hut and Domino's.

And the Winner Is . . .

The winner, in my opinion, is a slopegraph (Figure 4.63).

Bigger Slice
U.S. pizza chain market shares

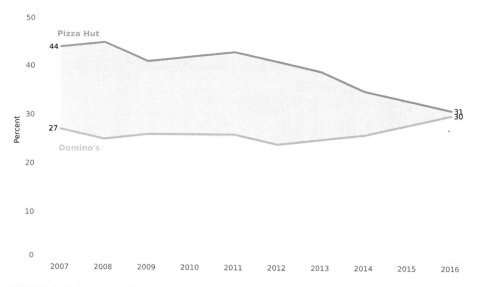

FIGURE 4.61 A line chart/area chart hybrid showing market share over time, accentuating the gap (data from Restaurant Research via Hedgeye).

---

* This technique of shading the gap was first employed by William Playfair in 1786. Playfair is credited with inventing the bar, line, area, and pie charts.

Bigger Slice
U.S. pizza chain market shares
Pizza Hut | Domino's

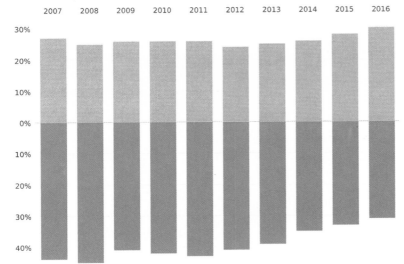

FIGURE 4.62 A divergent stacked bar chart that makes it hard to compare market share over time (data from Restaurant Research via Hedgeye).

Bigger Slice
U.S. pizza chain market shares

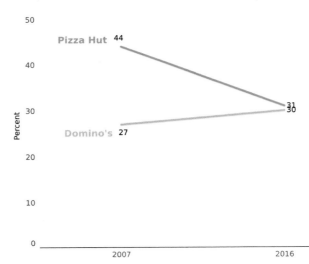

FIGURE 4.63 A slopegraph showing the starting and ending periods only (data from Restaurant Research via Hedgeye).

Here we show only the beginning and ending periods and skip the years in between. Yes, that's a judgment call, but given that there were no spikes or dips in the years in between, I think focusing on the start and finish makes a lot of sense.

Thinking Outside the Pizza Box

Here's another take on the data that shows the other players in the pizza chain market (Figure 4.64).

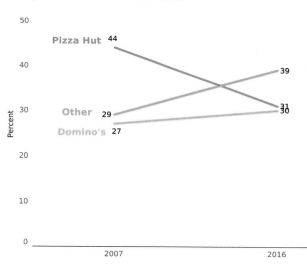

Bigger Slice
U.S. pizza chain market shares

FIGURE 4.64 A slopegraph showing the starting and ending periods only. Here we add Other into the mix (data from Restaurant Research via Hedgeye).

I can't take credit for this. When I created the assignment, I focused on the data from the *Wall Street Journal.* It was a workshop attendee, EJ Wojtowicz, who suggested that we were missing a very important insight: all the other brands combined are eating into Pizza Hut and Domino's market share.

This is yet another reason why I encourage workshop attendees to speak up and disagree with me. Good things happen when you have discussions about the data. The decisions about what data to include and what not to include are essential. We will discuss this more in Chapter 6.

Is It Ever OK NOT to Have the Value Axis Start at Zero?

Why do I (and many of my colleagues) think the charts in Figure 4.65 and Figure 4.66 are misleading?

But the charts in Figure 4.67 and Figure 4.68, which also truncate the value axis (meaning it doesn't start at zero), are fine. Let's look a little more closely to figure out why.

FIGURE 4.65 A misleading bar chart from a major news network in which the value axis does not start at zero (data from the U.S. Census Bureau, 2011; graphic reenactment by Randy Krum).

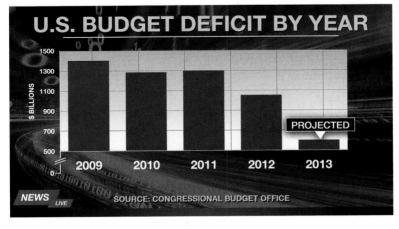

FIGURE 4.66 A misleading bar chart from a major news network in which the value axis does not start at zero (data from the U.S. Congressional Budget Office; graphic reenactment by Randy Krum).

Average Life Expectancy for the United States and Selected Countries, 1990–2018

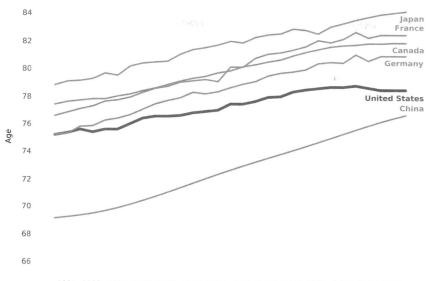

FIGURE 4.67 An honest line chart in which the value axis does not start at zero (data from the World Bank).

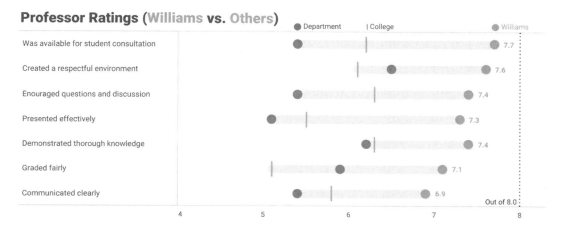

FIGURE 4.68 An honest connected dot plot comparing ratings for Professor Williams (teal) to other professors in the same department (dark gray) and to the college average (light gray line). Notice that the value axis begins at 4. (Based on Jeffrey A. Shaffer's Course Metrics dashboard from *The Big Book of Dashboards*.)

Continuing our analysis, why is the chart in Figure 4.69, which has the axis starting at zero, considered deceptive?

So why is the line chart in Figure 4.70 considered honest?

It might look like I'm cherry-picking based on my personal preferences and worldview, but there is good reasoning behind when it's OK and when it is *not* OK to truncate the axis—and you absolutely should know and understand it.

Let me explain why I think accentuating the temperature fluctuations is warranted, but instead of using global warming, let's consider another example. Suppose you want to monitor the temperature of little Billy, who is four years old. Billy lives in Europe, so we'll use the Celsius scale on which a normal temperature would be 37 degrees (98.6 F) and a high temperature would be 39.4 (103 F). If you start the value axis at zero, the chart looks like Figure 4.71.

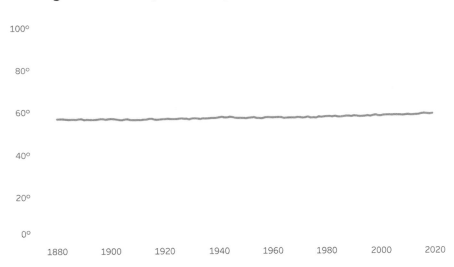

Average Global Temperature by Year

FIGURE 4.69 An intentionally misleading line graph that minimizes temperature fluctuations and also uses a value axis that starts at zero (data from NOAA National Centers for Environmental Information).

Average Global Temperature by Year

FIGURE 4.70 An honest chart that correctly accentuates the temperature fluctuations (data from NOAA National Centers for Environmental Information).

Billy's Temperature over 24 Hours

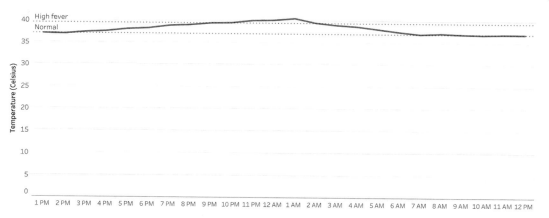

FIGURE 4.71 A line chart showing Billy's temperature over a 24-hour period using a 0 baseline.

Why start at zero? What does that have to do with a person's temperature? Figure 4.72 shows the same chart type starting at 35 degrees Celsius (95 F, which would indicate hypothermia), a much more logical baseline for this type of data.

To tie in with some of our discussions of color and preattentive attributes, I would probably indicate the period when Billy's temperature was very high using color as shown in Figure 4.73.

Billy's Temperature over 24 Hours

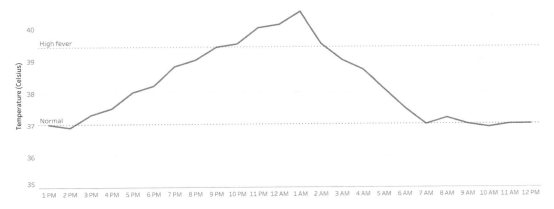

FIGURE 4.72 A line chart showing Billy's temperature over a 24-hour period using a more logical baseline. Note that Billy made a full recovery.

Billy's Temperature over 24 Hours

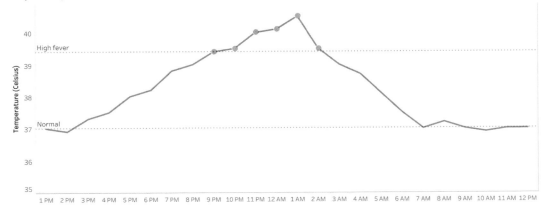

FIGURE 4.73 A line chart showing Billy's temperature over a 24-hour period using a logical baseline and color-coding the points when he had a high fever.

This same logic applies to the dot plot in Figure 4.68 where we saw the professor ratings for Professor Williams. No professor had a score below 4, and there's a big difference between a professor who has a 5.0 rating and one who has a 7.5 rating. The professor ratings dashboard accentuates these important differences, but a chart that had a value axis starting at zero would not.

Another important thing to consider: these are not bar charts!

It is never OK to have a bar chart not start at zero. Why? The consensus among data visualization experts is that with a bar chart, you are asking the audience to compare the lengths of the bars. This means they are predisposed to see that, for example, one bar is three times as big as another. Even if they notice the truncated axis, it's hard for them to shake their initial interpretation. With a dot plot or a line graph, you are asking people to compare the distance between the dots. Instead of just looking at the locations of the dots, they're more likely to think, "Look how big that gap is."

Sometimes, truncating the axis is warranted because it helps accentuate important differences, but other times it's done to bamboozle you (e.g., "Look how much sales have increased since last year!"). How can you tell the difference?

> If you see a bar chart where the value axis does not start at zero, your BS detector should be sounding an alarm.

If you see a bar chart where the value axis does not start at zero your BS detector should be sounding an alarm. Consider this seemingly innocuous bar chart, which appears to show a really big increase in sales (Figure 4.74).

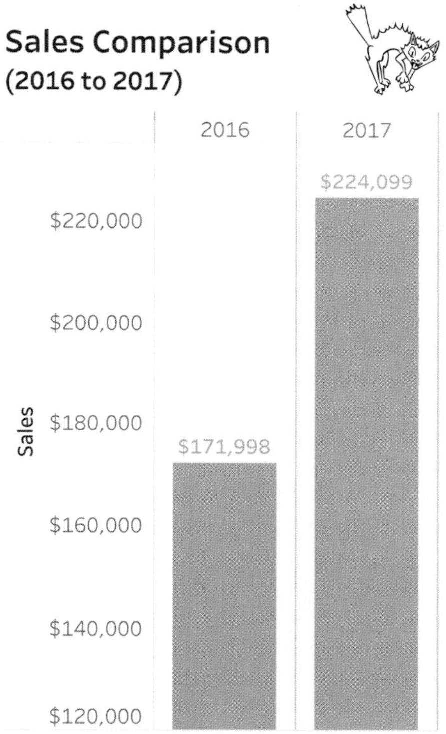

FIGURE 4.74 A misleading bar chart with a y-axis not starting at zero suggests sales have increased more than they really have.

Let's take away the numbers and just focus on the bars (Figure 4.75).

Just looking at the bars, the one for 2017 looks to be about twice as tall as the one for 2016. This is likely to be interpreted as meaning that sales doubled in 2017. Figure 4.76 shows the sales comparison using a value axis that starts at zero. This reveals that the sales increase was much more modest.

A word of caution: this doesn't mean that any dot plot, comet chart, or a line chart with a truncated axis will always be honest. Figures 4.77 and Figure 4.78 show how you can mislead people by overamplifying the difference between the two years.

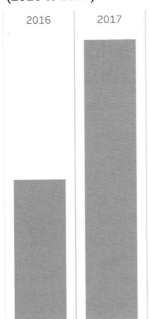

Sales Comparison
(2016 to 2017)

FIGURE 4.75 A misleading bar chart, with a focus on just the bars.

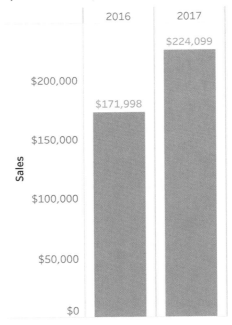

Sales Comparison
(2016 to 2017)

FIGURE 4.76 An honest bar chart with the y-axis starting at zero.

Perhaps you're asking, "Is there a rule we can follow?" I'm wary of establishing rules, as there are often reasonable exceptions. Instead, here are my guidelines:

- Truncating the value axis with a bar chart is almost always misleading.

- Truncating the value axis with a dot plot or line chart *may* be misleading.

- Truncating the value axis *may* be essential.

Look carefully. If you determine that you have, in fact, been hoodwinked, please push back on the person or people who created the chart. It may have been an honest mistake. Or they may prove to be an untrustworthy source of information.

FIGURE 4.77 Comparing honest versus dishonest line charts.

FIGURE 4.78 Comparing honest versus dishonest comet charts.

More "Axistential" Angst

In fashioning the jitterplot salary example earlier in this chapter, I grappled with whether I should start the value axis at zero or at $50,000, the lowest value in the data set (Figure 4.79).

I elected to leave the axis at zero, but would it have been deceptive to start at $50,000? What do you think?

(I think it would have been OK.)

MAPS

In Chapter 3 we saw some examples of filled maps and how they could help us compare life expectancy in different countries in Asia. There are many other types of maps with which people should be familiar, especially since filled maps (also called choropleth maps) often don't work well for comparing measures that are not related to the size of land area.

**Value Axis
Starts at Zero**

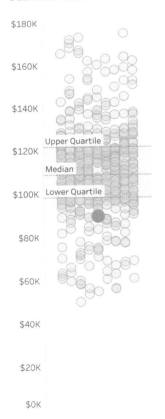

**Value Axis Starts
at Lowest Value**

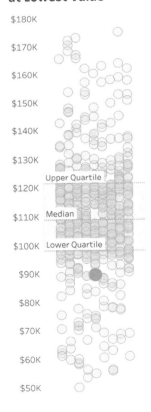

FIGURE 4.79 To truncate the axis or not to truncate the axis? That is the question.

We will explore several of these map types, but first, let's see why filled maps can cause problems.

Filled Maps

When I show people the map in Figure 4.80 and ask them to guess what it is about, practically everyone answers that it shows election results, with the red representing Republican areas and the blue Democratic locations. They then state that because there's so much more red than blue, this probably shows results from the 2016 election, in which Donald Trump defeated Hillary Clinton.

I then say that this is a county map showing the 2012 election in which Barack Obama (blue) defeated Mitt Romney (red). "How can that be?" they wonder. "There's so much more red than blue."

FIGURE 4.80 A filled county map showing the 2012 presidential election results for 48 of the 50 U.S. states. Alaska and Hawaii are not shown. Does the year surprise you? (Kelvinsong, Wikimedia Commons.)

I then show them the same election results, but by state rather than county (Figure 4.81).

It still looks like there is more red than blue, and if we added Alaska to the mix, there would be way more red than blue because Alaska is huge.

So why doesn't this work?

Maps are great for showing how much land there is, how that land is shaped, and the proximity of one location to another. It's not great at representing population, and the electoral college (the delegates that select the president) are a reflection of each state's population. For example, Montana has more land than California, but it has about 1 million people compared with California, which has about 37 million.*

Despite its popularity with news organizations, a filled map is not a great way to relate electoral college results. What might work better?

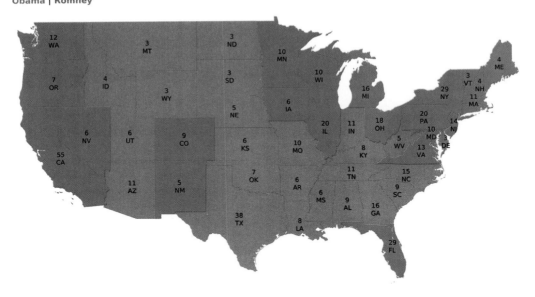

2012 Electoral College Results
Obama | Romney

FIGURE 4.81 A filled state map showing the 2012 presidential election results for 48 of the 50 U.S. states. Alaska and Hawaii are not shown.

---

* U.S. Census 2010. See https://www.census.gov/quickfacts.

For a thorough and entertaining exploration of how maps and other charts can be misleading, I encourage people to read *How Charts Lie* by Alberto Cairo.

Symbol Maps

Drawing circles on a map worked well in the mystery map example we saw in Chapter 2 (Figure 2.13). Maybe that would work here, too (Figure 4.82).

With a symbol map, workshop attendees report that they see more blue than red (and have an appreciation for the population of California when compared to that of Montana and Wyoming), but they still feel like it's a difficult comparison. What else might work?

Cartogram

A cartogram is a type of diagram in which we substitute land and distance with some other measure. Here's one attempt that uses a gridded cartogram/hexagram (Figure 4.83).

There are many more examples that work considerably better than the traditional symbol map and filled map. This begs the question:

2012 Electoral College Results
Obama | Romney

FIGURE 4.82 A symbol map showing presidential election results for 48 of the 50 U.S. states.

2012 Electoral College Results
Obama | Romney

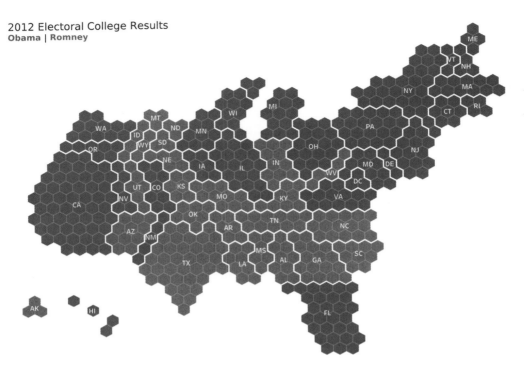

FIGURE 4.83 Electoral results from 2012 presented using a gridded cartogram/hexagram in which each hexagon represents an electoral vote (Ken Flerlage).

when do you need a *real* map, and when might a cartogram or other type of map work?

If you want to visualize anything having to do with land or distance, then a traditional map is the way to go. Otherwise, a cartogram or tile map may be a better way to go.

Here's a standard filled map showing the popularity of the most visited state park in each state in the continental U.S. between 2006 and 2016 (Figure 4.84).

You should be able to see that California and North Carolina had the parks that were

most popular. But what if you wanted to explore information about Rhode Island (RI), Maryland (MD), the District of Columbia (DC), or Delaware (DE)? Can you even find them? Because they occupy so little land mass, they are so tiny that it's hard to tell what color they are.*

Tile Maps

We could instead present the same data using a hexagon tile map (Figure 4.85).

---

* Anyone who does not live in the United States gets a pass on this one. And if you are wondering about Delaware, and why it's even harder to find than normal, the data is missing for that state.

Which States' Most Popular National Parks Were the **Most Visited** from 2006–2016?

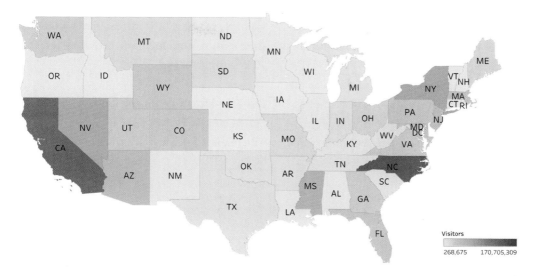

FIGURE 4.84 The popularity of U.S. national parks by state from 2006 to 2016 shown on a filled (choropleth) map.

Which States' Most Popular National Parks Were the **Most Visited** from 2006–2016?

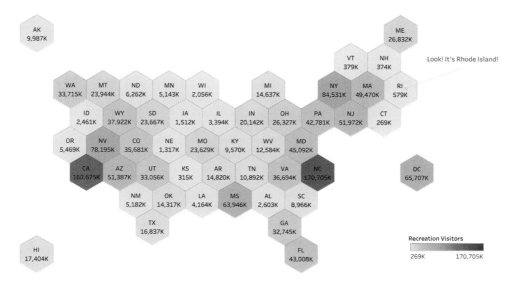

FIGURE 4.85 The popularity of U.S. national parks by state from 2006 to 2016 using a hexagon tile map.

Assuming you have a rough familiarity with the geography of the United States, it should be easy to find a particular state. Thanks to its compact form, this approach also makes it easier to include Hawaii and Alaska.

This tile map also allows us to display additional information that would be impossible to encode on a filled map. In this case, we've included the total number of visitors to each state's most popular park. Figure 4.86 is Matt Chambers's rendition of that same data. As you can see, Chambers has placed a timeline within each tile to show how attendance within each state's most popular park had changed from 2006 through 2016.

Do Tile Maps Work for Other Parts of the World?

Tile maps work for more than just the United States (although they fail for many European

FIGURE 4.86 The popularity of U.S. national parks by state over time, embedding an area chart within a tile map (data from the U.S. National Park Service, chart created by Matt Chambers, https://twitter.com/sirvizalot).

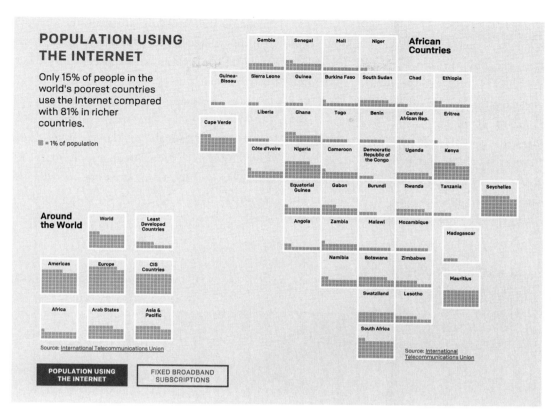

FIGURE 4.87 Percentage of population in different countries who have access to the internet (data from International Telecommunications Union, chart from ONE.org).

countries). Figure 4.87, published by the non-profit organization ONE in 2017, combines a tile map with another chart type. We haven't yet defined this second chart type, but study it for a minute or two and stretch your graphicacy skills.

Were you able to surmise that each turquoise square represents 1 percent of the population of the corresponding tile's country? If so, you are really coming along nicely. If not, no worries; we'll explore it together now.

This tile map is combined with a type of waffle chart. In this case, each tile contains a series of 10 by 10, dividing it into 100 small squares. For each small square that is filled in, 1 percent of the population of that country has access to the internet. While it's not as easy to make exact comparisons as in a bar chart, it works well here, where one large square demarks one country. You can get a rough sense of internet penetration by how many small squares each large square contains.

Treemaps

How else might we show the 2012 election results? Just because you have geographic data doesn't mean you must create a map. Figure 4.88 uses a treemap.

The treemap is a creation of professor and computer scientist Ben Shneiderman.* It's great for seeing the big picture when you have a lot of hierarchical data and two or more sub-categories. Here we have two categories that make up the hierarchy (Obama and Romney) and lots of sub-categories (the states).

There's also a bar chart that shows the overall electoral tally of 332 versus 206.

You may notice that some of the rectangles in the treemap are very small, so you cannot make out the state and the number of electoral votes. This chart is part of an interactive dashboard, so you can select any state from the list on the right and see just how much that state contributes to the whole (Figure 4.89).

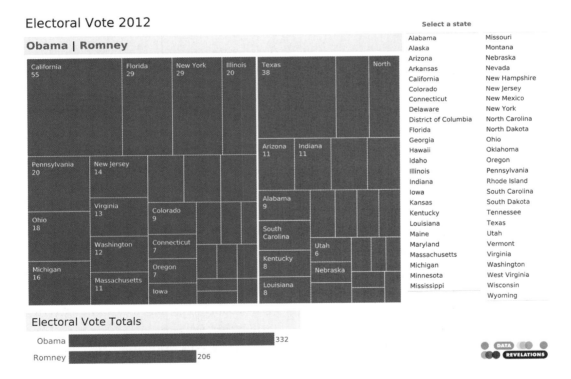

FIGURE 4.88 A dashboard featuring a treemap of the 2012 election results (Data Revelations).

---

* Shneiderman promotes an "information-seeking mantra" which is overview first, zoom and filter, then details-on-demand. In Chapter 9, you'll see lots of good examples that adhere to this ideal.

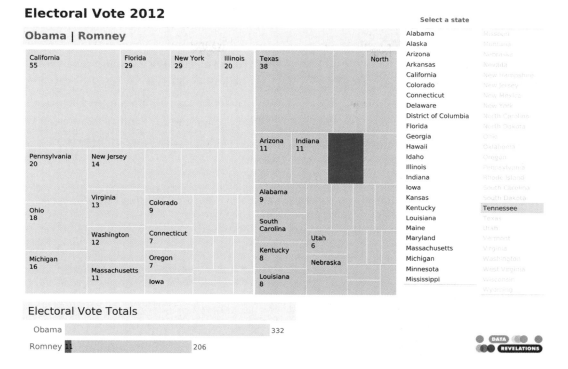

FIGURE 4.89 Interactivity allows you to select a state and see that state's impact on the election results (Data Revelations).

There is so much more to learn about maps than I can cover here. I strongly encourage you to watch the short but highly entertaining and enlightening video called "42 Amazing Maps," available at bigpic.me/42maps.

For those of you who are interested in seeing more approaches to displaying electoral votes, see "14 Ways to Visualize the Presidential Election" by Ken Flerlage at bigpic.me/election.

PIE CHARTS

Without question, the pie chart (and its cousin, the donut chart) are the most reviled by data visualization cognoscenti. You may be thinking, "Wait, why don't people like pie charts? I understand them without an explanation. What's the problem?"

The problem is that a pie chart does one thing well, and most people don't use it for that one thing. Specifically, they're great at giving you a fast and accurate estimate of the part-to-whole relationship for *two* of the slices. Other than that, pie charts are terrible.

And don't even think about comparing two pie charts side by side.

Let's explore this.

Consider the pie chart in Figure 4.90.

Some questions are easy to answer; for example, "Which slice is the largest?" Chairs. But lots of other questions are difficult, including ranking the slices or trying to figure out how much larger one slice is than another (more on that in a moment).

The one thing that pies are supposed to do well only works if the slice is in a certain location. Let's focus on Tables. Looking at Figure 4.91, can you figure out how large a percentage of the whole it takes up?

It's not so easy, but if we move that slice so it starts "at midnight" (Figure 4.92), we can see that it's just under one-quarter (23 percent to be exact).

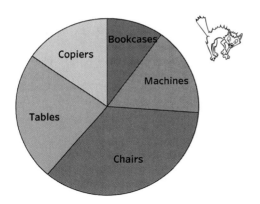

FIGURE 4.90 A pie chart divided into five segments.

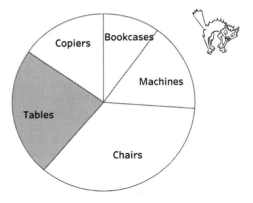

FIGURE 4.91 A pie chart comparing Tables with everything else.

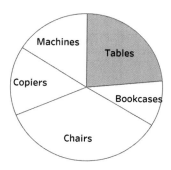

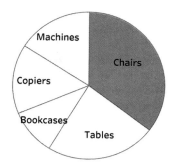

FIGURE 4.92 A pie chart comparing Tables with everything else, where the segment of interest, if you were to imagine a clock, starts at midnight.

FIGURE 4.93 A pie chart comparing Chairs with everything else, where the segment of interest, if you were to imagine a clock, starts at midnight.

If we try the same thing for Chairs, we can see with little effort that this slice takes up about one-third of the total (Figure 4.93).

Think back to the stacked bar charts we explored earlier in the chapter. For those, we could compare things only if they shared a common baseline. (Notice that I intentionally have not placed any numbers in the pie or bar charts so you can better gauge the strength of the visualization itself to help you make comparisons.)

When each segment starts at midnight, we can quickly see if something is one-quarter, one-third, and so on. That is why these brilliant measuring cups (Figure 4.94) can be read in an instant.

FIGURE 4.94 Measuring cups from Welcome Industries LLC.

Another problem with pie charts is that it's very hard to see how much larger one segment is than another. Look at Figure 4.95 and see if you can determine which is larger, Copiers or Machines.

Now compare the pie chart with a bar chart showing the same data (Figure 4.96).

It's easy to see that the bar for Machines is longer than the one for Copiers. We can also see that the bar for Chairs is about twice as long as the one for Machines.

Even so, the bars make it difficult to determine what percentage of the total any single

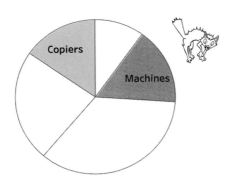

FIGURE 4.95 Trying to compare two slices that are of similar size using a pie chart is difficult.

Sales of Selected Catagories

FIGURE 4.96 A bar chart comparing the same five categories.

segment represents. (It's no easier if you add several segments together.)

This is why I like to combine bar charts and pie charts, so they can answer questions related to "Which is larger, and by how much?" and the "What is the part to the whole?" Consider the bar chart in Figure 4.97, which shows sales in 30 different states.

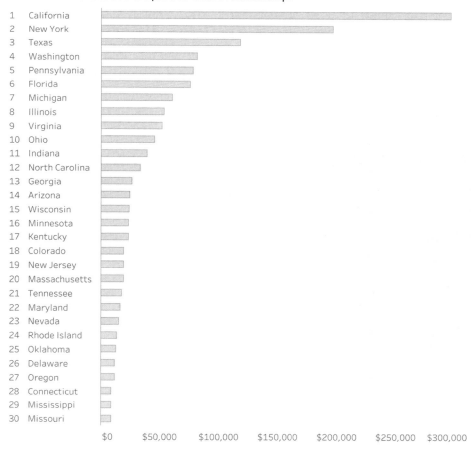

FIGURE 4.97 A sorted bar chart showing sales in 30 states.

Using an interactive dashboard, if we select California, the state with the highest sales, we can quickly see that it accounts for a little under 25 percent of sales (Figure 4.98).

Selecting several states will further show the part-to-whole relationship in a way that people can immediately see. In Figure 4.99, we see that the seven states account for a little under half of the total sales.

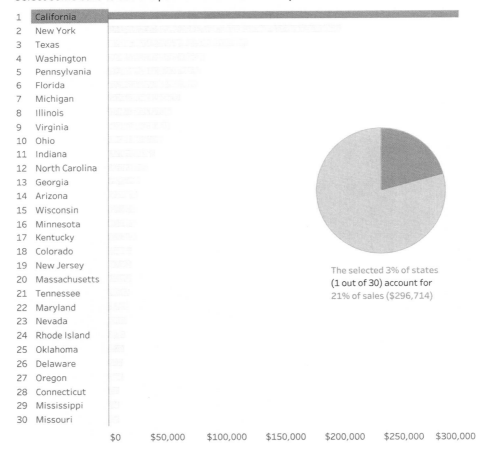

A Bar Chart and a Pie Chart Living in Harmony

Sales by State

Select some bars to see the part-to-whole relationship.

1	California
2	New York
3	Texas
4	Washington
5	Pennsylvania
6	Florida
7	Michigan
8	Illinois
9	Virginia
10	Ohio
11	Indiana
12	North Carolina
13	Georgia
14	Arizona
15	Wisconsin
16	Minnesota
17	Kentucky
18	Colorado
19	New Jersey
20	Massachusetts
21	Tennessee
22	Maryland
23	Nevada
24	Rhode Island
25	Oklahoma
26	Delaware
27	Oregon
28	Connecticut
29	Mississippi
30	Missouri

The selected 3% of states (1 out of 30) account for 21% of sales ($296,714)

$0 $50,000 $100,000 $150,000 $200,000 $250,000 $300,000

FIGURE 4.98 Selecting a state displays a pie chart showing the part-to-whole relationship.

A Bar Chart and a Pie Chart Living in Harmony

Sales by State

Select some bars to see the part-to-whole relationship.

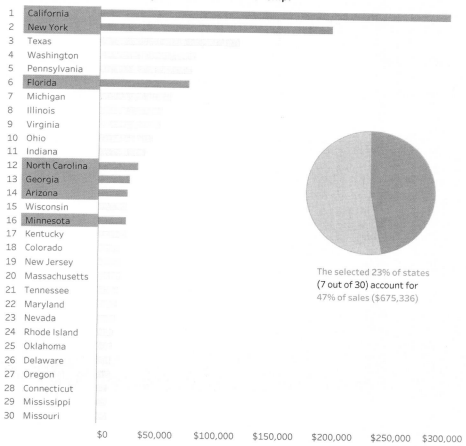

FIGURE 4.99 Selecting several states displays a pie chart showing the part-to-whole relationship.

If you enjoyed the discussion on the strengths (and mostly weaknesses) of pie charts, I strongly encourage you to read the very entertaining and enlightening essay "Save the Pies for Dessert" by Stephen Few (see https://bigpic.me/pies).

DONUT CHARTS

The same strengths and shortcomings that apply to the pie chart also apply to the donut chart. Consider Figure 4.100, where we show progress toward a goal (the full donut would represent 100 percent).

FIGURE 4.100 A donut chart showing progress toward a goal for a single segment (South).

This is an easy read. Even without the number in the middle, which is what people seem to love most about donut charts, it's easy to see that we're a little less than halfway toward our goal.

What happens if we have more than one region (Figure 4.101)?

This is a much more difficult comparison, and it would be even harder if the numbers were not in the center of the donut. Recall the recommendation to test the effectiveness of a visualization by removing the numbers. If a chart is difficult to decipher without visible numbers, it may not be that good a visualization.

Now, what would happen if one of the regions exceeded its goal? How do you show more than 100 percent with a donut chart?

The answer is that you can't, which is why the bar chart with a reference line is a much better choice for this situation (Figure 4.102).

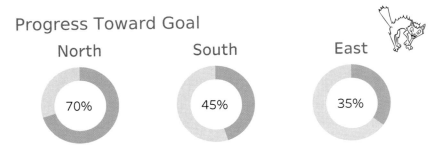

FIGURE 4.101 A donut chart showing progress toward a goal for several regions.

Progress Toward Goal

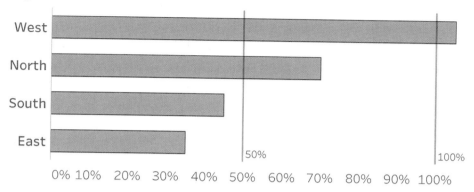

FIGURE 4.102 A bar chart with reference lines showing progress toward a goal for all the regions. Look at North and East. You can see that North is twice as long as East, which you cannot do with side-by-side-by-side donut charts.

Here are four guidelines (iron-clad rule and three recommendations):

1. Iron-clad rule: the slices/segments must add up to 100 percent.

2. If you are going to have a pie or donut chart, make sure it's just one pie or donut because comparing multiple pie charts is difficult.

3. If you are going to have more than two segments, make sure that the two segments you most care about each start at midnight, with one moving clockwise and the other going counterclockwise. In Figure 4.103 it's easy to see that Pemrose has a little more than half and Abdala is around

one-third because we have that common baseline reference point.

4. Never use 3D (and that goes for bar charts, too).

Candidate Choice

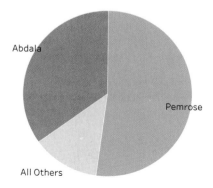

FIGURE 4.103 With a pie chart, only the segments that start at midnight are easy to estimate. The others are much more difficult.

BEWARE OF "XENOGRAPHPHOBIA"

Several years ago, I got a big kick out of this tweet from Maarten Lambrechts:

 Maarten Lambrechts
@maartenzam

Replying to @jburnmurdoch

@jburnmurdoch @monfera @eagereyes I'd say: make, publish and popularise them. They can be very powerful. Let's fight #xenographphobia

Avoid xenographphobia: the fear of unusual graphics/foreign chart types (Maarten Lambrechts via Twitter).

Xenographphobia! What a wonderful neologism meaning fear of unusual graphics.

Why do I bring this up? You should not be afraid to learn how to parse a chart that is unfamiliar. If you are a chart designer, you should not throw your hands up and exclaim, "Oh, our executive team will never understand that chart!"

Is the chart so complex or are the executives so closed-minded that they won't invest a little bit of time getting up to speed with an approach that may be new but very worthwhile? I'm not talking about novelty for novelty's sake (or because the designers are tired of making bar and line charts), but something that truly engages and better informs the audience.

I'll confess that I suffer from this problem as well. The first time I saw what I thought were some unnecessarily esoteric chart types, I thought, "What is this nonsense?" It turns out they weren't nonsense. It took all of 60 seconds for somebody to explain how the charts worked, and I immediately saw how valuable they were.

So What Should We Do?

For the person creating charts and dashboards, I've argued that you should always try to make it as easy as possible for people to understand the data, but you should not go crazy trying to make the perfect dashboard, nor should you oversimplify your visualizations. Simple is good; simplistic is not.

I also argue that while you should understand the skill set and mindset of your audience, you should not be afraid to educate them about new chart types, especially if it's the type of situation where they'll learn something once and use it over and over again.

If you are a consumer of the content, I hope you feel the same way. An investment of one minute of your time to understand how to read a chart may lead to hours of engagement and enlightenment.

CHAPTER 5

HOW TO GET PEOPLE TO USE CHARTS AND DASHBOARDS

If you were to look at an organization that has embraced data visualization, you would see some dashboards that people use regularly and others that, despite great effort and time spent by the developers, people avoid.

Why do people gravitate toward certain dashboards? Clearly, they are providing something the audience finds useful, but if you were to dig a bit more, you would find there's often an approach that makes these dashboards irresistible—and it isn't packed bubbles, word clouds, or charts with lots of curvy things.

It's *personalization* and, in particular, inserting the audience into the visualization.

What is the secret to getting people to use charts and dashboards? *Personalization.* Inserting the audience into the visualization, and making it especially meaningful and relevant to the user, never fails.

EXAMPLE 1: WHAT IS THE AGE DISTRIBUTION OF THE U.S. POPULATION?

Consider a histogram showing the age distribution of people living in the United States based on census data from 2019 (Figure 5.1).

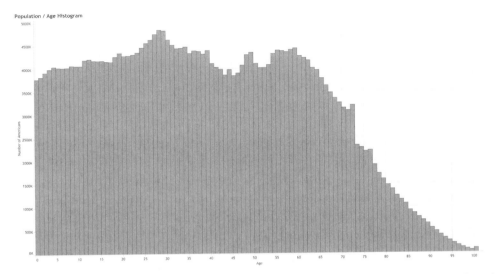

FIGURE 5.1 A histogram showing how many people in the United States are age 0 to 1, 1 to 2, and so on (data from U.S. Census Bureau).

I find this fascinating as I'm drawn to the big decrease around age 72, but when I show this to friends and family? Big snooze.

Curious about that big drop after age 72 in Figure 5.2? It's not that a large percentage of people start dying, but instead that so many more people were born between 1946 and 1967 (the Baby Boom generation).

Now, if we make the chart about the audience, people will use it, explore it, and most importantly, learn something from it. I've never failed to garner engagement when I show people this next example as they immediately select a bar to look at how their age compares to others (Figure 5.3).

And then they try their partner's age. Their kids'. Their parents'. Their older brothers' (I'm thinking about you, Rick).

Then they apply the filters.

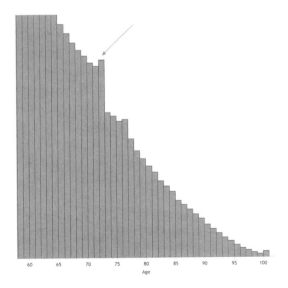

FIGURE 5.2 Why the drop-off after age 72? There were fewer people born before the Baby Boom (data from U.S. Census Bureau).

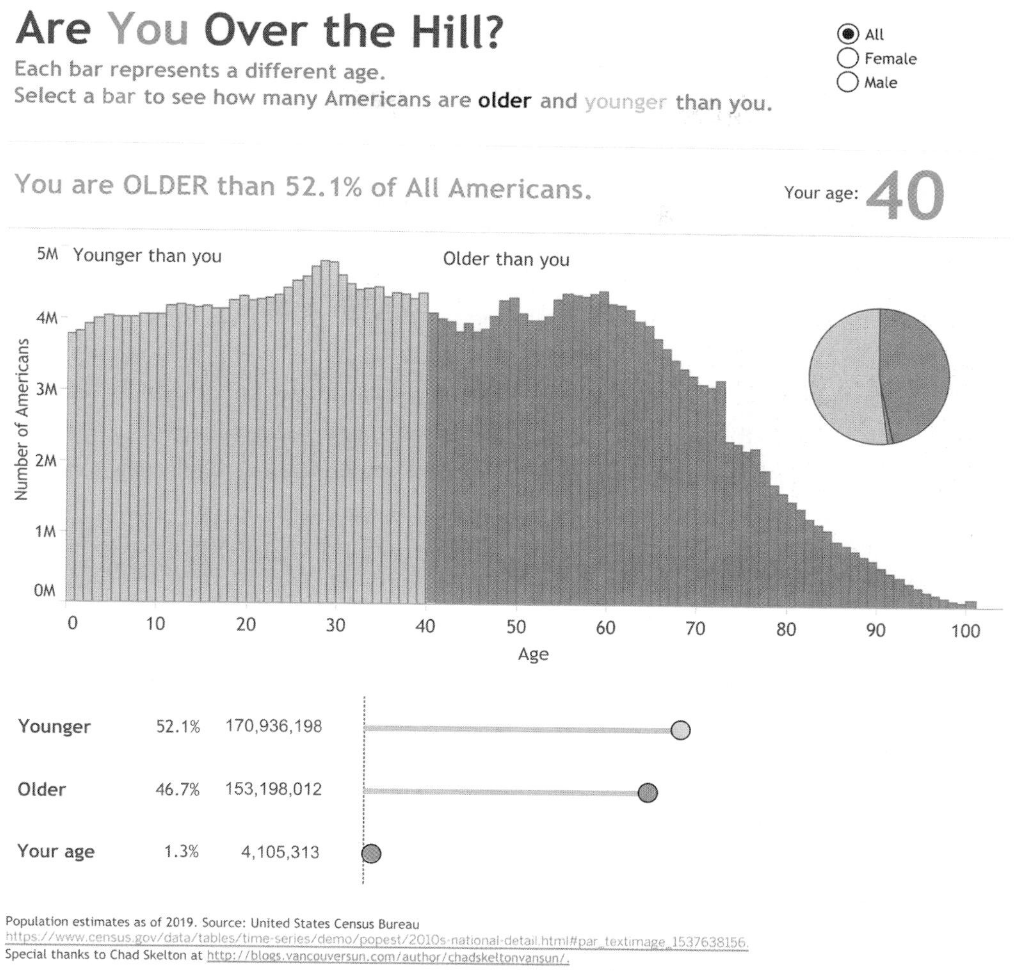
Are You Over the Hill?
Each bar represents a different age.
Select a bar to see how many Americans are older and younger than you.
All
Female
Male
You are OLDER than 52.1% of All Americans.
Your age: 40
Younger than you
Older than you
5M
4M
3M
2M
1M
0M
Number of Americans
0
10
20
30
40
50
60
70
80
90
100
Age
Younger 52.1% 170,936,198
Older 46.7% 153,198,012
Your age 1.3% 4,105,313
Population estimates as of 2019. Source: United States Census Bureau
https://www.census.gov/data/tables/time-series/demo/popest/2010s-national-detail.html#par_textimage_1537638156.
Special thanks to Chad Skelton at http://blogs.vancouversun.com/author/chadskeltonvansun/.

FIGURE 5.3 An interactive dashboard that allows people to see how much younger or older people living in the United States are (data from U.S. Census Bureau).

> Want to try this for yourself? Go to bigpic.me/age and see how much older or younger you are than people in the United States, but be prepared to be a little depressed if you are older than 50.

I've seen organizations do remarkable things when they make the audience the focus of a visualization. In the Introduction, we explored an example about the incidence of diabetes, but here are some other real-world examples that capture the audience's interest.

EXAMPLE 2: HOW HAS YOUR HOME PRICE CHANGED SINCE YOU PURCHASED IT?

The Federal Home Loan Mortgage Corporation, known as Freddie Mac, is a Fortune 50 company that buys mortgages on the secondary market, pools them, and sells them as a mortgage-backed security to investors on the open market. They maintain a massive amount of data about housing prices in the United States and make that available to the public.

Here's a table of data (Figure 5.4) showing how home prices have changed, by state, since 1975.

Assuming you purchased a home for $100,000 that year, how much more would your home be worth now? And what if you bought your home in 2011 and it cost more than $100,000?

How can you make this not just understandable, but something people would want to use?

Freddie Mac does a great job of making its data accessible with visualizations, many of which come from Leonard Kiefer, Freddie Mac's deputy chief economist. Inspired by Kiefer's work, Curtis Harris, Head of Analytics Engineering at Pluralsight, developed a personalized, interactive dashboard that allows anyone to select when they bought a home, the state they bought it in, and how much they paid for it (Figure 5.5).

Look at the dropdown items along the top. This person purchased a house in Nevada in October 2011 for $270,000. A home like that has

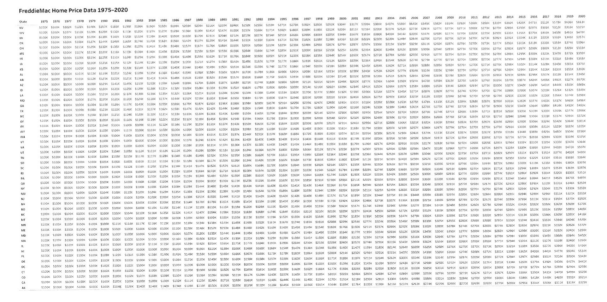

FIGURE 5.4 Freddie Mac housing price data (Freddie Mac).

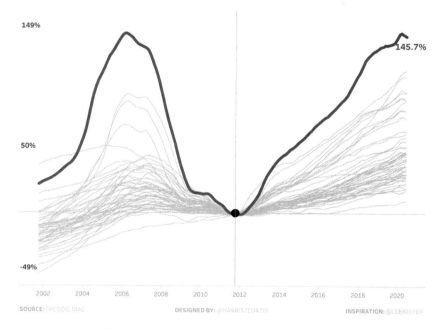

FIGURE 5.5 Personalized housing price information (Freddie Mac data, chart by Curtis Harris).

gone up in value almost 150 percent. Talk about buying at the right time!

There's a massive amount of data packed into a very small space, but it's clear and elegant because it only shows what is relevant to the audience: information about him/her.

Each line represents a different state, but only the user's state is highlighted. If you want to explore a different state, you certainly can, and it would answer questions like: "We almost moved to North Carolina in 2008. What would that house we considered buying then be worth now?"

Also notice that Harris doesn't show house prices going back to 1975. He's intentionally constrained the lookback period to 10 years because limiting the amount of data shown in this case makes it more pertinent to the user's interests and makes it easier to understand because there's less information to process.

EXAMPLE 3: HOW IS THE STORE I MANAGE DOING COMPARED WITH OTHERS?

This example is a mashup of work I've done for a major U.S. retailer and a global hotel chain. In both cases, the entities wanted to make it easy for managers to see how their properties were doing compared with other properties.

In Figure 5.6 we see a personalized dashboard that shows the manager responsible for store S34 how it is doing compared with other stores. Note that every manager gets this personalized view in which his or her dot is the centerpiece of the story.

The manager of this store will likely be concerned because the store received an overall score of 6.1 out of 10 and is ranked 14 out of 15. It's easy to see that this store is performing poorly with respect to Cleanliness, Staff knowledge, and Had what I wanted (just look for the green dots that are significantly lower than the other dots.)

This is a chance for the manager's manager (e.g., the director) to help improve performance.

You may be thinking, "Goodness, I would not want the public humiliation of everyone being able to see how poorly my store is performing." Realize that in this example nobody except the director and senior management knows which dots belong to which stores. As a manager, you can see that there are other stores, with some doing well and some doing poorly, but you cannot tell which stores (other than your own) each dot represents.

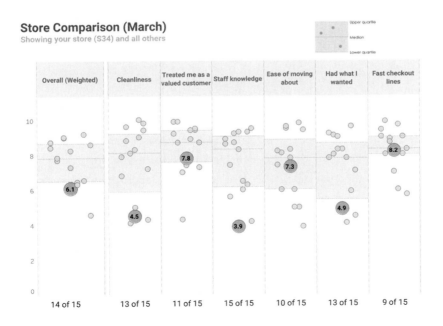

FIGURE 5.6 Store comparison dashboard for March.

If I were the director, I would look at which stores were doing well and consider having the managers of those stores confer with the manager of store S34. I'd also create clear goals and incentives to improve performance. Imagine how good the manager will feel if a month later he or she managed to move the dots, as shown in Figure 5.7.

The organization may reach a point at which *all* stores are performing well, even the store ranked last. In that case, it would make more sense to compare store performance against some other quantifiable measure, such as improvement from the previous year.

Note: Every time I've seen this type of comparative dashboard used, it has resulted in underperformers striving to do better. Yes, it can be

upsetting to see your dot in a bad location, but it can be uplifting to see its placement improve over time. That is *exactly* the type of impact you want to have with data visualization.

EXAMPLE 4: HOW IS OUR STATE DOING WITH STUDENT AID APPLICATIONS?

In the United States, FAFSA (Free Application for Federal Student Aid) completion is a key indicator of a high school senior's plan to attend college and an important factor in financial aid offers, so it is a critical metric for college access organizations and high schools to track. The National College Attainment Network (NCAN) is a

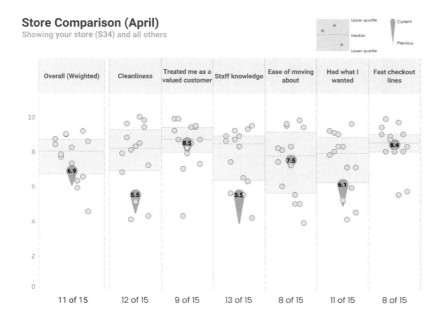

FIGURE 5.7 Store comparison dashboard for April.

not-for-profit organization whose mission is to build, strengthen, and empower communities and stakeholders to close equity gaps in post-secondary attainment for all students.

NCAN tracks a massive amount of data, including FAFSA completion rates for each state. In Figure 5.8, we see a dashboard using their data that would allow an educator or interested party from a state to see that state's rankings.

Jenn Schilling, a data scientist and consultant to the Arizona Commission to Postsecondary Education, and her colleagues looked at this dashboard with a focus on their state (Figure 5.9).

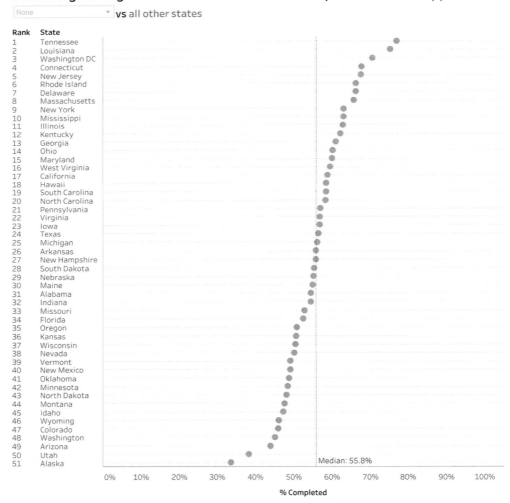

FIGURE 5.8 FAFSA completions by state, as of July 2020 (National College Attainment Network).

Percentage of High School Seniors That Have Completed a FAFSA Application

Arizona ▾ **vs** all other states

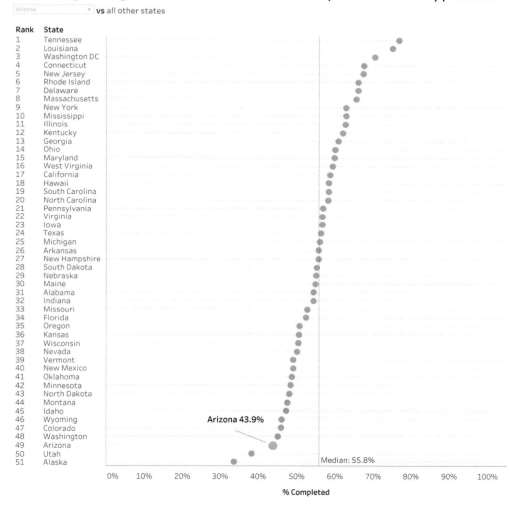

FIGURE 5.9 FAFSA completions with a focus on Arizona (National College Attainment Network).

We see that Arizona currently ranks 49th in the United States for FAFSA completion rates of high school seniors. Since millions of dollars in federal financial aid are left on the table each year by students not completing the application, the Arizona Governor's Office of Education, the Arizona Commission for Postsecondary Education, and Achieve 60AZ partnered to create the Arizona FAFSA Challenge. This statewide initiative aims to increase FAFSA completion among Arizona high school seniors. As a resource to assist with tracking FAFSA completion, Schilling built a collection of interactive dashboards that act as a vital resource for high school staff, administrators, and community stakeholders to view the FAFSA completion progress for the state and for the hundreds of individual Arizona high schools monitored.

How do you make it easy to see how your school is performing compared with 400 other schools? Figure 5.10 shows an attempt to make it possible and easy.

There are 400 schools represented in this visualization with each dot representing one school. Dots toward the bottom (1) have a low completion rate. Dots toward the top (2) have a high completion rate.

The goal is to be above 52 percent (3).

Large dots have a high enrollment of high school seniors, while small dots have a low enrollment (4). Dark blue dots mean a school's completion rate is much higher this year than last year. Dark orange means a school's completion rate is much lower than last year (5).

Note that Covid-19 resulted in many schools having fewer in-person FAFSA events

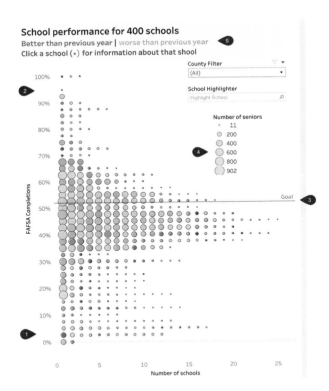

FIGURE 5.10 FAFSA school comparison dashboard for Arizona (FAFSA).

in the spring. It also undermined the ability of college-access professionals to work one-on-one with students to make sure they completed their FAFSA applications. One can still compare FAFSA completion rates in the 2019–2020 school year to those in 2018–2019, but it's important to understand that some schools may have much worse results than last year due to the pandemic.

Let's imagine you are the superintendent, principal, or a college advisor for Maryvale High School (Figure 5.11). The first thing you might

do is use the school highlighter to find Maryvale (1), then select it (2) to see how it got to be where it is today (3 and 4).

We see that Maryvale is still hitting the state-wide goal, but it is down quite a bit from the previous year (3). The difference chart (4) is another way of showing this year versus last year, and represents the year-over-year differences for the same time period. Maryvale started this year ahead of last year, dipped, rallied, and dipped again.

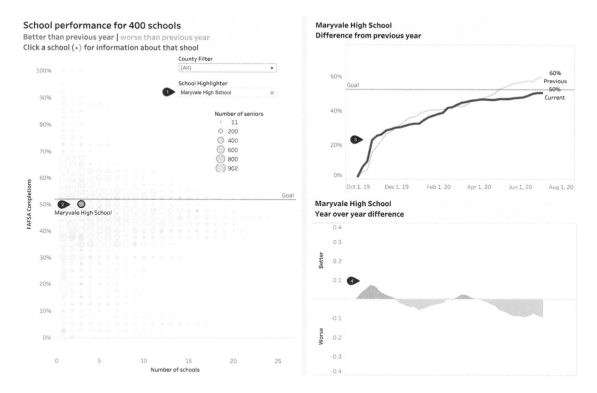

FIGURE 5.11 Maryvale High School's FAFSA completion compared to those of other schools and compared to the previous year (FAFSA).

After inspecting my own school, I would be interested in seeing which schools with a similarly sized student body did much better than last year and which did worse. One can look for a similarly sized blue dot and find a school that did particularly well. Figure 5.12 shows FAFSA completion rates for San Luis High School.

Likewise, we can click a dark orange dot to look at FAFSA completions for a school whose rate declined from the previous year, as we see with Camelback High School in Figure 5.13.

All of these examples have one thing in common in that they show where the things you care about are with respect to the big picture.

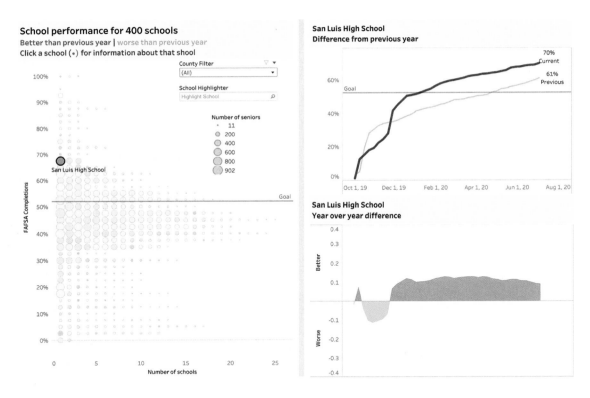

FIGURE 5.12 FAFSA completion rates for San Luis High School (FAFSA).

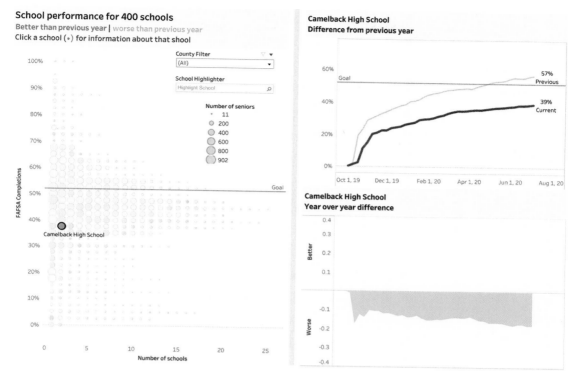

FIGURE 5.13 FAFSA completion rates for Camelback High School.

> The best way to engage people and drive adoption is to provide something useful and meaningful, and one of the best ways to do this is to make it *personal*.

WHAT DOES YOUR AUDIENCE WANT?

Years ago, a friend recommended I read Kathy Sierra's *Badass: Making Users Awesome.* The thing I was supposed to glean from reading this was that "people don't want to be badass at using your tool. They want to be badass at what your tools help them do."

That was not my takeaway. Instead, the book got me thinking about my workshops and presentations. How is what I present going to help the person who is in the audience? If it's not going to help, why am I showing it? What is it that the audience wants to know?

This now informs everything I do. I make a joke of showing attendees a typical agenda slide (Figure 5.14)...

Typical Agenda Slide

8:30 – 9:00	Breakfast
9:00 – 10:30	Fundamentals of database design
10:30 – 10:45	Break
10:45 – 12:00	Hands-on exercises
12:00 – 1:00	Lunch
1:00 – 2:30	Introduction to object-oriented databases
2:30 – 2:45	Break
2:45 – 5:00	Hands-on exercises
5:00	Workshop end

FIGURE 5.14 A typical agenda slide.

. . . followed by an agenda slide that is more in tune with what the audience wants to know (Figure 5.15).

This gets a nice chuckle because everyone in the audience thinks, "Yes! That's *exactly* what I was looking for!"

Agenda with Audience Needs in Mind

8:30 – 9:00	Breakfast
9:00 – 10:30	Blah blah blah blah blah
10:30 – 10:45	Break
10:45 – 12:00	Blah blah blah blah blah
12:00 – 1:00	Lunch
1:00 – 2:30	Blah blah blah blah blah
2:30 – 2:45	Break
2:45 – 5:00	Blah blah blah blah blah
5:00	Happy hour

FIGURE 5.15 A more audience-centric agenda slide.

But then I see an *aha* moment as the attendees realize that I was really thinking about what they were interested in, and I hope they will start to think about this (if they weren't already) in their own work.

To the visualization creators, I don't want to dissuade you from making things that are beautiful. Just realize that if what you build isn't meaningful, your audience won't use it.

To the visualization consumer and influencer, do not fall into the trap of thinking that fancy dashboards are going to improve adoption. They may attract interest at first, but if they make things harder to understand, people will abandon them.

The best way to engage people and drive adoption is to provide something useful and meaningful, and one of the best ways to do this is to make it *personal*.

CHAPTER 6

WHY COLLABORATION

IS CRITICAL

In my consulting work I've seen a huge number of data visualization and dashboard initiatives fail. Almost all of these failures had something in common: the developers didn't understand what the audience needed, and the audience didn't understand what the developers built.

Here's how you can avoid this.

Had you told me not that long ago that I would advocate building a dashboard by committee, I would have said you were crazy. I was convinced that business data visualization was a me-only activity and I should only surface when I had questions about the data.

I've completely changed my thinking on this as I've seen much better results when people collaborate than when they build things independently.

Let me share two case studies, a workshop epiphany, and some insights into why the Allies won World War II.

CASE STUDY 1: CUMULATIVE FLOW

Several years ago, Troy Magennis, president of Focused Objective LLC, called me to ask if I would help him build embedded dashboards for a Nashville-based client and train their employees. Troy is an expert in software development modeling and probabilistic forecasting.

The goal of the project was to supplant visualizations like the cumulative flow diagram shown in Figure 6.1 with dashboards that would provide significantly better insights.

Here's my memory of the phone call:

Steve: So, how will this work?

Troy: These are smart people, and they know the data very well. They just don't know data visualization very well.

You would come in and help one or two people on the team build some prototype dashboards, and then train the users, marketing team, and senior management who would participate in designing the dashboards.

Steve: Wait, you mean we're going to create dashboards by committee, with everyone giving his or her opinion on what would be the best charts and colors?

Troy: I don't know if I would call it that, but we want to get feedback and incorporate good suggestions into the design and implementation.

Steve: O . . . K . . . [I was thinking of something a little stronger.]

I'll admit I thought this was a horrible approach, as I envisioned senior management insisting on 3D pie charts with nauseating colors (sorry for the image that is now in your head).

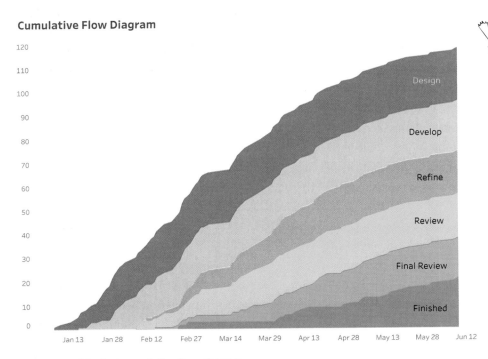

FIGURE 6.1 A typical cumulative flow diagram.

Boy, was I wrong! Troy led a clinic on how to engage with stakeholders, quickly iterate, and turn stakeholders into active collaborators who would later promote adoption once the dashboards were released.

Let's see how this worked.

In my first meeting, I worked with Troy and a dashboard developer, and we built a working prototype. We then presented our case to all the stakeholders (people who would use it, sell it, and market it), explaining why what we had was better than the current approach.

This was a great chance for me to educate people not steeped in data visualization on pre-attentive attributes, effective use of color, why bar charts rule, and so on. Note that this was about teaching, not showing off. It was also a chance for *me* to be schooled, as I got to see things from the stakeholders' perspectives. They let me know what was unclear, as well as the needs and challenges they had in using the dashboards and driving adoption.

So what happened after our 30-minute jam session?

I caucused with Troy and the developer for a few minutes, and we indicated that we would need 60 minutes to implement their feedback into a new version of the dashboard. Yes, that's all it would take as the developer knew the data and we had a tool that would allow us to iterate—fast!

Sixty minutes later, we met again. This time we got much closer to the goal of getting the stakeholders to think "Ah, now I see this really clearly."

After the meeting, we said that we would have another revision for them the next day (some of the modifications would take time to implement) and moved on to a different dashboard.

Over the two days, we created some really good stuff. For me, it was helpful to see things through fresh eyes. For the stakeholders and collaborators, they were able to see why the visualizations they had clung to were not as clear and easy to interpret as they had thought. Realize that we didn't say, "Obviously, our stuff is better." Instead, we asked, "Which dashboard makes the questions we have easier to answer? The one you had with the cumulative flow diagram or the one that we're building together?"

Another amazing thing happened: the stakeholders, now coauthors, took pride in the new dashboards. They would later become the most ardent supporters when the new dashboards were rolled out. Think: "Look how great this is! And by the way, I helped design it."

CASE STUDY 2: CHURN

Several years ago, a client asked about a good way to show churn. Human resources departments are often tasked with seeing what areas of their companies are hiring or losing people. Likewise, organizations that offer subscriptions services (e.g., gyms, magazines, streaming services) need to track how many people are signing up and how many are leaving. (This data is further broken down by as many demographics as you can imagine.) This was right around the time I was immersed in writing *The Big Book of Dashboards* with Jeffrey Shaffer and Andy Cotgreave (and that was a good thing, as we'll see in a moment).

Figure 6.2 shows a simplified version of the data the client wanted to understand.

Here's how to interpret this: The company first opened its doors in January, and 210 people signed up for the service. In February, 245 people signed up, but 150 decided not to renew,

resulting in a net of 95 subscribers for the month and an overall total of 305 subscribers.

In March, 270 people signed up, but 87 decided not to renew, netting 183 subscribers that month and leaving the organization with a total of 488 subscribers.

I looked at this and thought "waterfall chart," which is not something you see very often and which we hadn't seen earlier when we looked at 30 different chart types.

	Gained	Lost	Net	Running Total
January	210	0	210	210
February	245	-150	95	305
March	270	-87	183	488
April	320	-87	233	721
May	290	-178	112	833
June	209	-190	19	852
July	200	-200	0	852
August	263	-191	72	924
September	282	-91	191	1,115
October	264	-148	116	1,231
November	195	-120	75	1,306
December	280	-102	178	1,484
Total	3,028	-1,544	1,484	1,484

FIGURE 6.2 Simplified churn data.

Here was my first attempt to come up with something that would make it easy to see who was signing up and who was leaving (Figure 6.3).

My next 30 attempts were equally unsuccessful. Showing churn proved to be more difficult than I had anticipated! Fortunately, I had stakeholders (the client and my book coauthors) who pushed me to come up with something that got people to *aha!* (Figure 6.4).

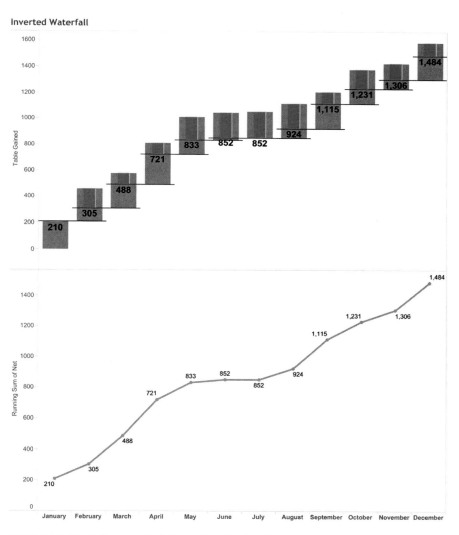

FIGURE 6.3 First attempt at building a visualization that shows churn.

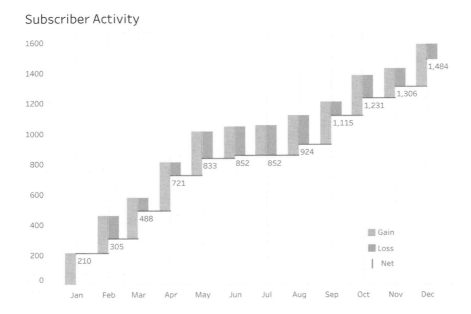

FIGURE 6.4 The *aha!* waterfall chart.

Not sure how to read this? This is a case where the best chart for the job is something that my audience may never have seen before, and I'm going to have to teach them how to read it. Fortunately, it's easy and I can explain it in under 30 seconds (watch the video at bigpic .me/churn to see for yourself).

This approach nailed it for the client and is featured in *The Big Book of Dashboards*, but

I never would have gotten something that worked as well for my intended audience without collaborating and iterating with my stakeholders.

WHY I ENCOURAGE PEOPLE IN MY WORKSHOPS TO DISAGREE WITH ME

In my dashboard design workshops, I present a hands-on exercise where attendees use pens and sticky notes to visualize this data set (Figure 6.5).

Before and After

Percentage of students that agreed with each statement before course and after course

Question	Before Course	After Course
Enjoy being in nature	15	97
Spend more time outdoors	48	98
Want to study science	45	92
Want to use science in everyday life	62	97

FIGURE 6.5 Percentage of people surveyed who agreed with the statement before taking a course and after taking a course.

We review everybody's work and then I show folks some approaches I would take to visualizing this data set. I start with the one in Figure 6.6, a gap chart. (We discussed this in Chapter 4. It goes by many names, including a connected dot plot, a dumbbell chart, a barbell chart, and a Cleveland plot.)

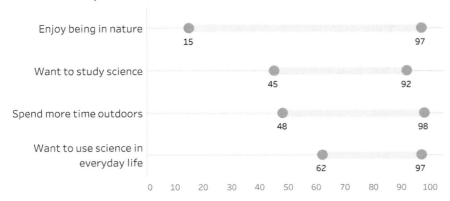

Percentage of Participants Who Agree with Each Statement

Before course | After course

FIGURE 6.6 Before and after data presented using a gap chart.

The previous image (Figure 6.6) is my preferred approach, but I make sure to show what I think are viable alternatives, including the one shown in Figure 6.7.

And because I am the expert with the really cool presentation clicker (and it is a *seriously* badass clicker), people nod and think, "Oh, I guess that's good."

The next day is typically a sequence of master classes in which I work with small teams to help them implement the theory of the workshop in their dashboards. On one of these second days, before we started the session, one participant, Ivana Ferrer, said she had a problem with the distributed slope area chart in Figure 6.7. Ferrer found it confusing because she thought she was being asked to compare the area of four trapezoids.

Yikes. She had a point.

I was very comfortable with the distributed slope area chart, so I expected others would be, too. I was not seeing my visualizations through fresh eyes.

I followed up and asked if a simpler distributed slopegraph (Figure 6.8) would be less confusing, and she said it worked well for her (other people in the group agreed).

Lesson learned. Just because something may be clear to me doesn't mean it will be clear to others. Now, at the beginning of all my workshops, I encourage participants to disagree with me because it paves the way for good discussions (and better dashboards).

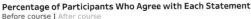

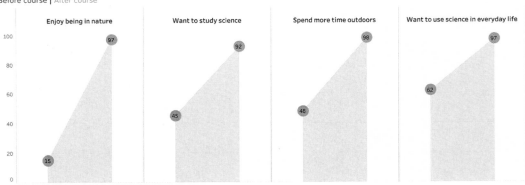

Percentage of Participants Who Agree with Each Statement
Before course | After course

FIGURE 6.7 A distributed slope area chart.

Percentage of Participants Who Agree with Each Statement
Before course | After course

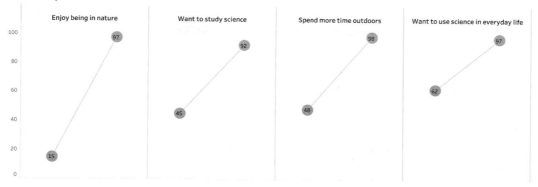

FIGURE 6.8 A distributed slopegraph.

THE DEVELOPMENT OF RADAR IN WORLD WAR II

In *Loonshots*, author Safi Bahcall recounts how Vannevar Bush, the head of the Office of Scientific Research and Development, spearheaded the rapid development of game-changing technologies, including radar. Without radar, the Allies almost certainly would have lost the war.

But the adoption of aircraft radar was turbulent. Bahcall writes:

No product works perfectly the first time. If feedback from the field is ignored by inventors, initial enthusiasm can rapidly fade, and a promising program will be dropped. Early aircraft radar, for example, was practically useless; pilots ignored it. [Vannevar]

Bush made sure that pilots went back to the scientists and explained why they weren't using it. The reason had nothing to do with the technology: pilots in the heat of battle didn't have time to fiddle with the complicated switches on the early radar boxes. The user interface was lousy. Scientists quickly created a custom display technology—the sweeping line and moving dots now called a PPI display. Pilots started using radar.

I want to stress that the pilots spoke directly with the scientists. There was no intermediary. I bring this up because I've seen organizations in which there isn't direct communication between developer and audience, and this often impedes improvement and adoption.

THE INGREDIENTS FOR SUCCESS

What do you need on your team to succeed with rapid data visualization iteration?

- Somebody who **knows the data and the subject matter.**

- Somebody who **knows what visualizations would work well** with the data (i.e., the data viz expert).

- **Stakeholders who have skin in the game,** meaning that they will either personally use the dashboard or are responsible for successful dashboard adoption. No, the stakeholders will not have their collective heads down, working on the visualizations that will be cranked out over the one or two days of rapid iteration. They will, however, need to be ready to meet for the 30–45-minute feedback sessions over the course of the engagement.

- A data visualization tool that allows you to **iterate quickly**. This could be a rapid development data visualization tool like Tableau or Power BI, or a whiteboard and colored markers.

- A **facilitator that steers the discussion** and makes sure it doesn't get bogged down. I've done this while also being the data viz person, but it's better when somebody else handles this. I suggest you hire Troy, who is *great* at this.

- **No jerks.**

I don't mean to be flippant with that last item, but your initiatives will fail if you have a key person who digs in his or her heels and insists on doing things a certain way, even though it's clear that certain visualizations are easier and faster for people to understand.

This gets to a key difference between making business visualizations and creating art. When I was working on *The Big Book of Dashboards*, friends asked me how I avoided fights with my fellow authors, Jeffrey Shaffer and Andy Cotgreave. We never had fights, but we did have great discussions and debates, and these debates led to better work.

This is because we weren't a rock band having artistic differences because one of us wanted to play jazz. We were completely aligned in having a common goal: to provide the greatest degree of understanding with the least amount of effort.*

---

* Of course, we mean the least amount of effort for the audience; the developers may have to put in a lot of effort.

If you engage with your stakeholders properly, they can be your collaborators, and together, you will make better visualizations, faster.

Collaboration isn't me saying *red* and you saying *blue* and us agreeing on *purple*. That's compromise. Collaboration is when we make something together that is better than what either of us would have made separately.

> We were completely aligned in having a common goal: to provide the greatest degree of understanding with the least amount of effort.

WHAT'S IN IT FOR YOU?

The designer: I can't think of anything more frustrating than working hard to build something, only to discover that people aren't using what you built. This happens all the time! Meeting early (and often) with your stakeholders and producing several iterations will reduce the likelihood of this happening, as you won't go too far down a path before realizing you are way off course.

The stakeholder: Think about that report or dashboard that you found dense and unhelpful. Chances are, several people in your organization worked really hard on it. What a waste of time! And it will happen again if you don't get involved early (and often) and help make clear what is useful and what is not. These get-togethers (plural) do not have to be long drawn-out affairs, and they can lead to you a great set of tools to help you and people throughout the organization make better decisions, faster.

People who want to learn and up their game: Maybe you are one of many people in your organization who is supposed to use the chart or dashboard and you simply don't get it. Others probably feel the same way but don't want to appear ignorant. Please, please, please ask somebody to explain the chart to you. If you do this, one of two things will happen: someone will show you how the chart works, why it's so valuable, and you will have a new and helpful tool; or you'll discover that all of your colleagues are also flummoxed and, together, you may be able to petition the design team (or the people who manage the design team) to collaborate with you so you can all have a tool that is useful.

> Collaboration isn't me saying *red* and you saying *blue* and us agreeing on *purple*. That's compromise. Collaboration is when we make something together that is better than what either of us would have made separately.

CHAPTER 7

HOW DASHBOARDS AND INTERACTIVITY LEAD TO BETTER INSIGHTS

Imagine you need to get up to speed quickly with something that would normally require a minimum of four hours of research, if you were to do it on your own. Fortunately, a colleague has prepared a detailed brief that provides you with everything you need to know and takes you just 15 minutes to read from start to finish.

The brief is terrific, and it answers most, but not all, of your questions. Fortunately, the colleague is armed with something that can answer many of the questions not explicitly addressed in the brief.

Or, suppose you attended a presentation. You were convinced it would be 60 minutes of torture but instead it was 20 minutes of incredibly useful, curated findings with great charts that made it easy for you to understand the data that was presented. The person who put it together did a stellar job of anticipating the needs of the audience but, as good and thorough as the presentation was, there were some questions at the end that had not been addressed. Like the writer of the brief, the presenter was armed with a potent tool to answer many of the questions that came up.

What did the brief writer do to distill four hours of research materials into 15 minutes? How did the speaker curate key findings into a tight, enlightening presentation? How did they both address questions not directly discussed in the brief or presentation, while providing a tool that would allow their audiences to explore things on their own?

They were each armed with a good dashboard and the ability to interact with it to address questions, explore different avenues, and discover new insights.

THE CASE FOR INTERACTIVITY AND SELF-SERVICE

I fervently believe that organizations would benefit greatly from less printing and more clicking. I've got nothing against printing a document if that document answers my questions.

But if I need to see more details, or if I want to answer questions not addressed in what I had printed, a self-service chart or dashboard can be a game changer.

Let's see how this works.

Figure 7.1 shows one of the slides from the hypothetical presentation I referenced earlier. In this case, the presenter had sifted through a lot of scenarios and determined that her audience would find this insight particularly useful.

The audience in my example did in fact love this slide as the Ladders category was a hot topic for the people in the meeting. But one attendee wanted to know about the line at the bottom (the worst performing category), and another attendee wanted to know about the line

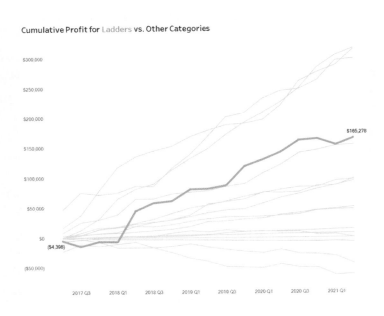

FIGURE 7.1 A slide from a well-curated presentation.

at the top (the best performing category). Fortunately, the presenter anticipated that people might ask questions like these, so she accessed her interactive chart during the Q&A and answered the questions immediately (Figure 7.2).

More importantly, she showed the stakeholders how to use the dashboard to answer these questions themselves. A huge benefit of interactivity is that the decision makers using a dashboard can experiment and help curate what's important to glean new insights. It's not solely up to the chart creator to decide what is important.

What would she have done if she didn't have interactivity? I've seen many organizations prepare a slide deck with 17 different versions of that same visualization, one for each category. In fact, I've seen organizations prepare massive, 500-page slide decks to show results for all combinations of categories, regions, divisions, and so on. This is a ridiculous amount of work for something that can be answered *instantly* with interactivity.

No Interactivity Invites Clutter

I often see chart creators place numbers on every bar in a bar chart and every point on a line chart. I'll ask the designer why he or she did

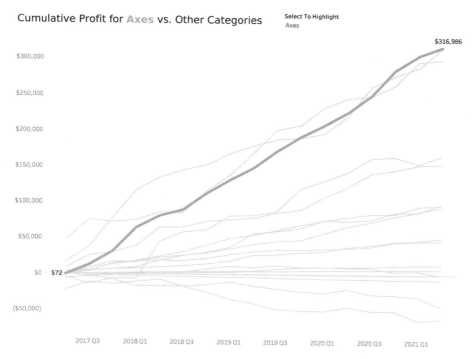

FIGURE 7.2 Exploring a category not covered in the presentation.

this, and the response is almost universally that the stakeholder asked to see all the numbers.

Marking everything on a chart may allow the stakeholder to see every number, but it also adds a lot of clutter (Figure 7.3).

People really don't need to see every number to be able to compare values, see trends, or derive insights. I think the alternative approach in Figure 7.4, in which only the highest and lowest values are marked, is much easier on the eyes.

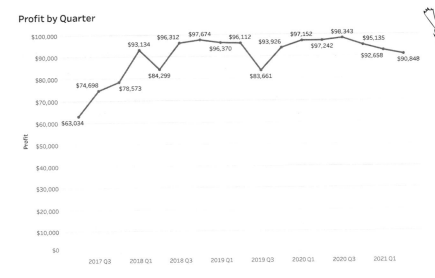

FIGURE 7.3 Showing the numeric value of every point on the line clutters the chart and makes the chart harder to understand.

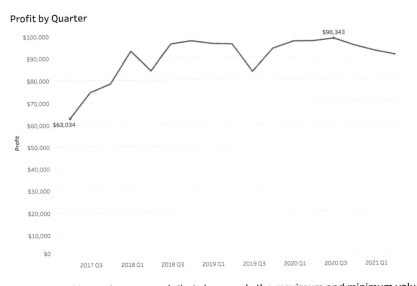

FIGURE 7.4 Alternative approach that shows only the maximum and minimum values.

In an interactive environment, if the audience really wants to see the details about a particular mark, they can simply hover over that mark (Figure 7.5).

Period: 2019 Q3

Profit: $83,661

$98,343

FIGURE 7.5 With interactivity, hovering over a mark will display details about that mark.

More Interactivity Examples

In Chapter 4, we explored the problems with a stacked bar chart. With a stacked bar chart, the two things people can easily discern is whatever is along the baseline and the overall total. *Without interactivity* the dashboard designer must hope that he or she has correctly guessed what is most important to the audience. *With interactivity* the order of elements can be changed on demand. Consider the example in Figure 7.6 where the focus is on the West region.

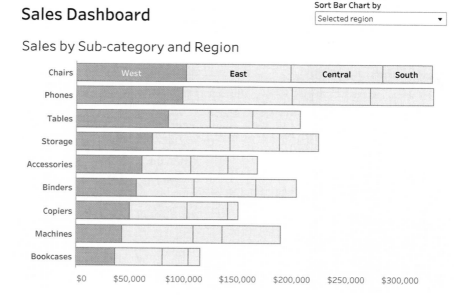

FIGURE 7.6 Stacked bar chart with a focus on the West.

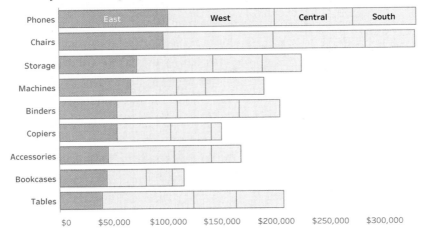

Sales Dashboard

Sort Bar Chart by
Selected region ▾

Sales by Sub-category and Region

FIGURE 7.7 Stacked bar chart with a focus on the East.

A user can click East, and the order of elements and the product sub-categories will re-sort, as shown in Figure 7.7.

Suppose the user wants to see the bars sorted by *overall* sales and by the selected region? Interactivity would allow that, too (Figure 7.8).

Here's another example. Consider the *Financial Times* index chart comparing Covid-19 cases in different countries. The online version is interactive, so people can select different countries and apply different settings (see top of Figure 7.9).

THE CASE FOR DASHBOARDS

As the author of a book on how to design dashboards I'm biased on the subject, but I think a good dashboard can be invaluable in helping organizations understand their data and monitor their operations.

Just what is a dashboard? Here's the definition my fellow authors and I proposed in *The Big Book of Dashboards*: A dashboard is a visual display of data used to monitor conditions and/or facilitate understanding.

Sort Bar Chart by

FIGURE 7.8 Sort drop-down selection gives the audience control.

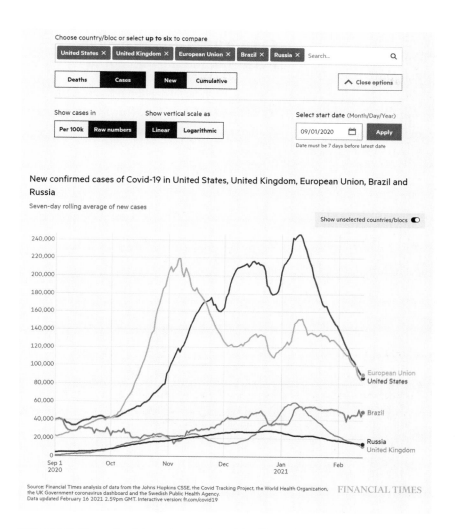

FIGURE 7.9 The online interactive version of the *Financial Times* index chart allows the user to select which countries to compare and which settings to apply. (*Financial Times* / FT.com, February 17, 2021. Used under license from the *Financial Times*. All rights reserved.)

Yes, this is a broad definition, and there is no discussion of explanatory versus exploratory, static versus interactive, fits on one screen versus scrolls, one chart versus several, drills down to another screen, and so on. I acknowledge that having clear definitions of all the different variations can help dashboard designers better manage the expectations of dashboard consumers, but I do not want to get into those specifics and semantics. For now, I want to discuss how useful a dashboard can be to reveal important insights that might otherwise have remained hidden. I also want to show how you often need more than one chart to connect all the dots—and a dashboard can be an amazing dot connector!

Case Study 1: Understanding Performance and Volatility

Figure 7.10 shows a dashboard currently in use at a global investment firm. The sectors and fund names have been anonymized.

Let's explore the individual components and see how they work together.

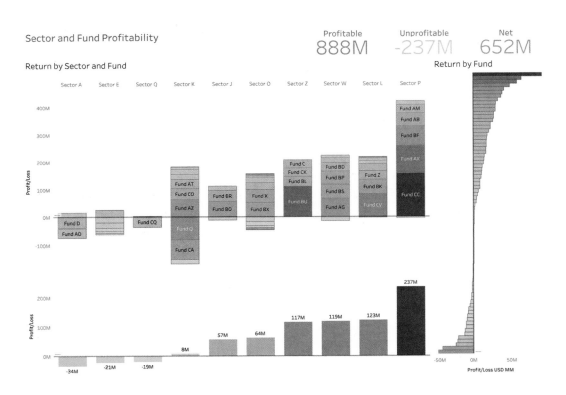

FIGURE 7.10 Hedge fund dashboard.

Return by Sector and Fund

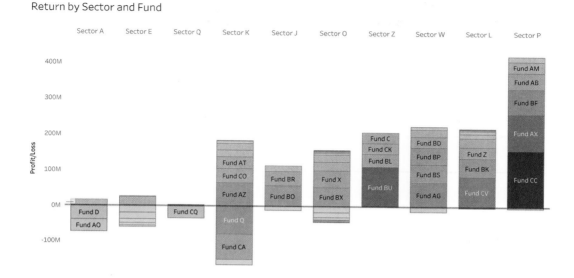

FIGURE 7.11 Return by sector and fund.

Figure 7.11 allows us to see the overall profitability and unprofitability of the funds by sector. We can easily compare the heights of the combined orange bars with each other, and the heights of the combined blue bars with each other. We can also see which sectors have a lot of funds and which have few, as well as get a sense of which ones are really pulling their weight (a big blue bar), or dragging things down (a big orange bar).

This is a good start, but suppose we want the overall profit, or lack thereof, for each sector? We need to add another chart (Figure 7.12).

We can see in Sector K (1) that even with some funds losing money, the sector overall is turning a profit. But suppose we want to compare each fund's profit or loss, independent of sector. We need another chart (Figure 7.13).

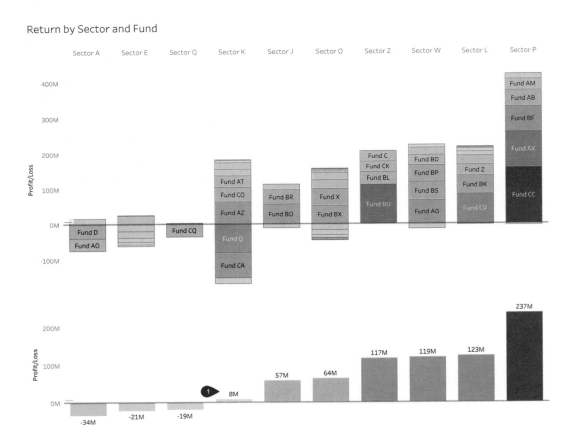

FIGURE 7.12 Return by sector and fund, and overall profit or loss for each sector.

Return by Fund

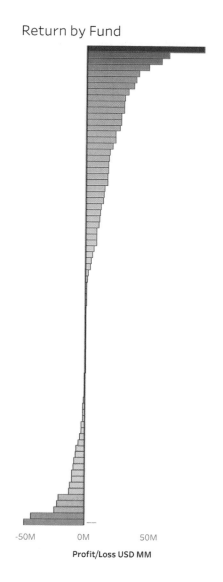

-50M   0M   50M

Profit/Loss USD MM

FIGURE 7.13 A tornado chart showing the profit or loss for individual funds.

Putting It All Together

Let's see what happens if we want to explore Sector K (Figure 7.14).

Selecting Sector K (1) highlights its individual funds in the tornado chart and reveals that the two least profitable funds are in this sector (2). It also filters the key performance indicators (KPIs) at the top of the dashboard (3).

This dashboard answers a lot of questions, but it also *poses* a lot of questions—and that is a good thing! For example, regarding the two lowest performing funds: Was that always the case, or is this a new development? Who is responsible for managing these funds? How are this person's other funds doing? A good dashboard should help you answer questions, but it should also start discussions about issues that you may not have considered.

FIGURE 7.14 Using interactivity to reveal insights.

BANs (Big-Ass Numbers)

Profitable	Unprofitable	Net
888M	-237M	652M

FIGURE 7.15 An example of BANs.

BANs (big-ass numbers) are large, occasionally overstuffed KPIs. Prior to working with Jeffrey Shaffer and Andy Cotgreave on *The Big Book of Dashboards*, I tended to look at them as ornamental rather than informational. I thought they just took up space on a dashboard without providing much analysis.

I've changed my mind and now recommend their use to my clients. Consider how helpful they are in our hedge fund example (Figure 7.15) as they provide some key take-aways (profitable funds, unprofitable funds, and net numbers) along with a color legend (blue = profitable, orange = loss).

In this case study, we showed how several coordinated charts helped provide insights. In the next one we'll see how applying the right filters and layers can reveal insight from a single chart.

Case Study 2: Deriving Insight from a Single Chart

Direct Relief is a nonprofit, humanitarian supply chain organization based in Santa Barbara, California. As the novel coronavirus began its spread at exponential speed throughout the world and across the United States in early 2020, Direct Relief had to scale and target its medical supplies like never before in its 72-year history. Their scope of support included access to personal protective equipment (PPE) to keep frontline health workers safe, essential medications for intensive care units, medical aid for health centers and clinics experiencing unprecedented medical pressures, and tens of millions of dollars in grant resources to keep the U.S. healthcare safety net functioning.

In this example, we'll look at a Covid-19 tracking dashboard built by Sidney Drill, Lindsey Turcotte, and Dalton Ruer from Qlik, and Andrew Schroeder from Direct Relief. It allows an analyst to identify high-risk populations that do not have immediate access to a hospital facility, indicating that they might be in greater need of resources.

The dashboard gives the analyst four controls for overlaying different views, including two that highlight hot spots and identify populations that may need resources (Figure 7.16).

Color Map By:

| Population |
| **% Population Over 65** |
| % Population with Diabetes |
| Flag: Top 10 Percentile 65+ |
| Off |

COVID-19 Heatmap

| Total Known Cases |
| New Cases Today |
| **3 Day Rolling Growth Rate** |
| Cases per 100K |
| Off |

FIGURE 7.16 Using map layer controls to identify vulnerable populations and where cases are growing (Direct Relief, data from Johns Hopkins, the CDC, and Definitive Healthcare).

In Figure 7.17, we identify hotspots based on three-day rolling case rates per state, combined with a filled map showing the percentage of the population over the age of 65.

The hotspot indicator combined with the darker background color indicate problems in Montana (1) and Florida (2). Yes, there are other hotspots, but it is the combination of hotspot and a dark filled map (indicating a large population over the age of 65) that is of greatest concern.

Let's zoom in on Montana (Figure 7.18).

We now see the counties that make up the state of Montana, still colored by the percent

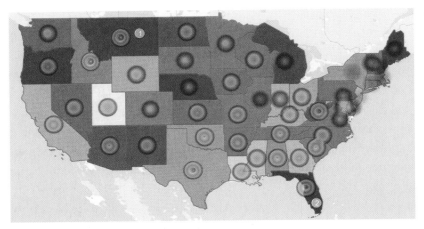

FIGURE 7.17 Hotspots on a filled map of the contiguous 48 U.S. states, showing a three-day rolling case rate combined with percentage of the population over 65 (Direct Relief, data from Johns Hopkins, Centers for Disease Control, and Definitive Healthcare).

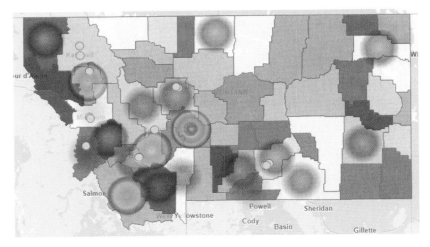

FIGURE 7.18 Hotspots on a filled map of Montana counties showing a three-day rolling case rate combined with the percentage of the population over 65 (Direct Relief, data from Johns Hopkins, Centers for Disease Control, and Definitive Healthcare).

of the population over 65, and hotspots show-ing Covid-19 growth rates. Notice in the upper left, Lincoln County, fits our criteria for a glow-ing hotspot and a dark filled map representing a high elderly population.

Where are the nursing homes in Lincoln? Are there hospitals close by? Again, the dash-board controls allow the analyst to overlay nursing home locations (circles) and hospital locations (triangles). (See Figure 7.19.)

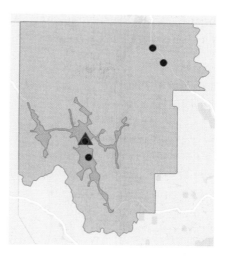

FIGURE 7.20 Superimposing a 45-minute drive time layer. Anything in the purple area is within a 45-minute drive (Direct Relief).

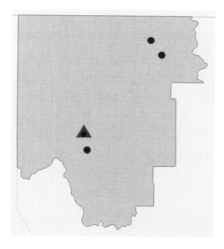

FIGURE 7.19 There are four nursing homes (circles) and one hospital (the triangle, obscuring one of the circles) in Lincoln (Direct Relief).

Are the two nursing homes located in the northeast of the county within a 30-minute drive of the hospital? A 45-minute drive? Again, dashboard controls allow the analyst to over-lay a drive-time view to see what portions of the county are within the requested drive time of the hospital (Figure 7.20).

Note that the odd-shaped purple layer shows locations that are within a 45-minute drive from the hospital. We often see circles rep-resenting areas within a 5-mile radius, 10-mile radius, and so on, but those are as the crow flies. Looking at real-world drive times is much more useful and, in this case, shows that there are two nursing homes that are particularly vulnerable. The next step would be for the analyst to look at the area near the two nursing homes outside of the 45-minute drive area to find partners that could receive necessary supplies to address ill-nesses locally.

This is a great example of being able to monitor conditions and, using interactivity, discover important insights and act. But what about the idea that a dashboard can be used specifically to facilitate understanding, and that it may never even be seen by stakeholders?

Dashboards Facilitate Understanding

Makeover Monday is an online learning project. Each week, participants are asked to explore an existing visualization and data set, and are then tasked with coming up with alternative ways to present the same data. It's a great way to practice data visualization and see how others tackle visualizing a common data set.

Figure 7.21 shows a snippet of the data from an example from several years ago.

I participated that week. Figure 7.22 shows the visualization I built.

I would never publish this. OK, I *did* publish this, but would not expect anybody to act or be moved by what I built in this instance. I made

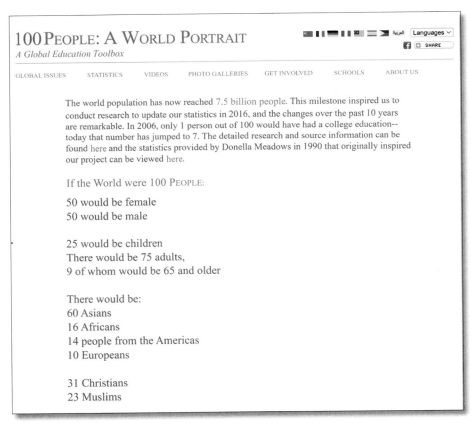

FIGURE 7.21 A portion of a data set from a Makeover Monday exercise (100people.org).

If the World Were 100 People

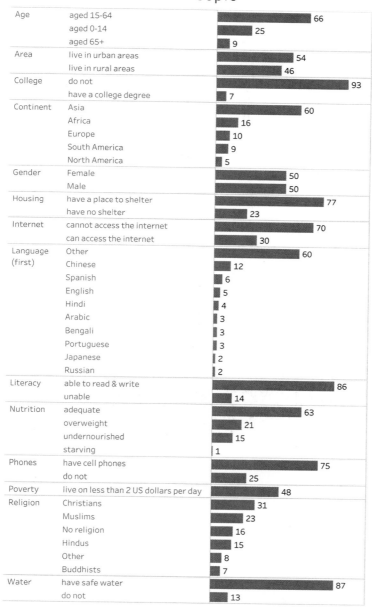

If the world had just 100 people this would be the breakdown by various demographics.

Based on data from
http://www.100people.org.

I spent some time looking at the source data and it appears to come from well-vetted sources. That said, please do not make any conclusions without satisfying your own "reliability threshold."

Design: @DataRevelations
http://www.datarevelations.com

#MakeoverMonday week 48 (2017)

FIGURE 7.22 My rather uninspiring Makeover Monday submission.

the dashboard *simply to help me understand the data.*

So what might I do with it, now that I see the big picture? What facet might I want to highlight, and what story might I want to tell?

Maybe I want to focus on nutrition (Figure.7.23).

What does it mean that 1 out of 100 people is starving?

Here's what Athan Mavrantonis did with this data (Figure 7.24).

FIGURE 7.23 Focusing on the 1 out of 100.

FIGURE 7.24 Athan Mavrantonis's stark—and stunning—visualization (Athan Mavrantonis).

Beware of Facts Without Context

Mavrantonis's visualization is thought-provoking. Should we be alarmed or encouraged?

You may be wondering how anyone could be encouraged by such a sobering statistic?

You need to look at it in a historical context. As bad as this number is, the prevalence of starvation and undernourishment is less than it was 10 years ago and considerably less than it was 25 years ago. It's the improvement that is encouraging.

The need for context with facts about the world is a major thesis of Hans Rosling's wonderful book *Factfulness*. I'll have more on Rosling and his book a little later.

This is a simple, elegant, and very powerful visualization. Indeed, you don't need to create something complex to have an impact.

This visualization is also beyond my design abilities. Had I wanted to create something like this for a magazine, I might have hired somebody with Mavrantonis's skills—but only after I first had a solid understanding of the data.

Most of my clients are creating visualizations for internal use within an organization.

Sometimes I assist with visualizations that are customer facing, but very rarely do I build something for a general-purpose audience. If you see me ditching bar charts in favor of something with a greater design aesthetic, it's because *I thought about who my audience is and what I want them to know (and feel).*

Knowing one's audience is essential.

It's also the focus of the next chapter.

CHAPTER 8

WHY KNOWING YOUR AUDIENCE IS ESSENTIAL

used to watch *Night Gallery* when I was a kid. It was an anthology TV show from Rod Serling, the creator of *The Twilight Zone*. I remember one episode in which the bad guy dies and goes to hell. He ends up in a waiting room with a bunch of bumpkins who want to share their vacation slides while listening to truly vapid music. Our protagonist tells the attendant that he can't stand the boredom of the waiting room and can't wait to get to the fire and brimstone and suffering. More time goes by and he again exclaims, "Hey, enough with this waiting room. When do I get to see hell?"

The attendant, who turns out to be Satan, explains that, "Hell is never what you expect it to be. But for you, this is it. It's a curious thing,

but they have the exact same room up there (gesturing toward heaven). You see, while this room is absolute Hell for you, up there it is someone else's idea of heaven."

This episode reminds me of an interesting debate about one of the sacred cows of data visualization.

CHARLES MINARD'S DEPICTION OF THE LOSS OF TROOPS IN THE RUSSIAN CAMPAIGN OF 1812–1813

Edward Tufte, data visualization scholar and author of several books, writes in *The Visual*

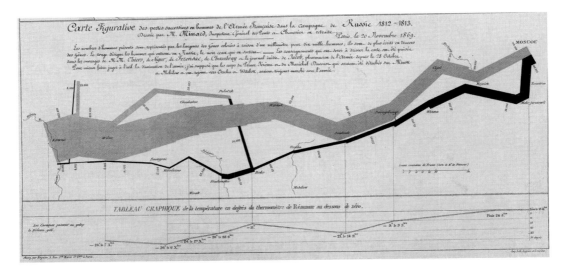

FIGURE 8.1 Charles Minard's 1869 "Figurative Map" of Napoleon's campaign to conquer Russia in 1812–1813. (Ecole nationale des ponts et chaussées, Fol.10975, https://patrimoine.enpc.fr/document /ENPC01_Fol_10975.)

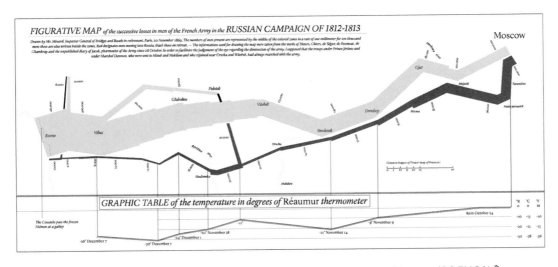

FIGURE 8.2 An English-language rendering of the Minard chart (Iñigo Lopez Vazquez/CC BY-SA).*

---

* There's a lot of debate as to whether when the original version was published the thick tan-colored lines were in fact red, and that the color has faded over time. Indeed, the text that accompanies the chart reads "Red designates men moving into Russia, black those on retreat." In *Beautiful Evidence*, Tufte argues that the ink has not faded and provides evidence from other charts Minard created. Norbert Landsteiner, who has spent a lot of time analyzing the chart (and even built an online interactive version) makes a strong case that the original had a reddish hue that has faded (see https://www.masswerk.at /nowgobang/2018/observing-minard). For our purpose, the shading does not matter.

Display of Quantitative Information that the chart shown in Figure 8.1 "may well be the best statistical graphic ever drawn."

Before we go any further, let's see a modern rendering of this in which the words have been translated into English (Figure 8.2).

I don't know anyone who, upon first seeing this chart, understands how to read it, but given that so many people hold this up as the *Mona Lisa* of charts, it's worth taking a few minutes to decode.

Let's start by seeing the geographical focus of this flow map by superimposing the image on top of a modern map (Figure 8.3).

The Journey to Moscow

Napoleon begins his campaign in Kovno (Kaunus), Lithuania. The thick line in Figure 8.4 (shown in tan) represents the number of troops. Napoleon begins with a staggering 422,000 troops!

FIGURE 8.3 The Minard image overlaid on a modern map.

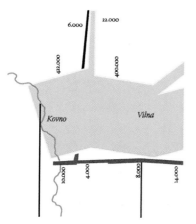

FIGURE 8.4 The thick tan line at Kovno shows the beginning of the campaign. The thin black line shows the end of the campaign. We will ignore the black lines for the time being.

Most of the troops head east, toward Vilna, but 22,000 troops head north . . . and wait.

The march continues in Figure 8.5, with some troops heading north and then east to Polotsk, but most marching east. Notice that the line is growing thinner, indicating that Napoleon is losing troops to disease, hunger, battle, and desertion.

Eventually, Napoleon reaches Moscow, but with only 100,000 troops. As we saw earlier, some headed out of harm's way (at least temporarily), but the loss of life was staggering as the Russians employed scorched-earth tactics,

destroying towns and crops and pressuring the French supply chain beyond its capacity.

Rather than surrender, the Russians burn Moscow to the ground. Napoleon waits a month for a peace offer from Emperor Alexander I that never comes. It's now mid-October, and Napoleon has no choice but to withdraw.

The Retreat

In Figure 8.6 we focus on the much thinner black line (1) along with a reverse timeline chart at the bottom (2) that shows the temperature during the retreat (3).

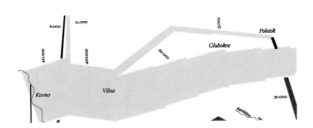

FIGURE 8.5 The campaign continues.

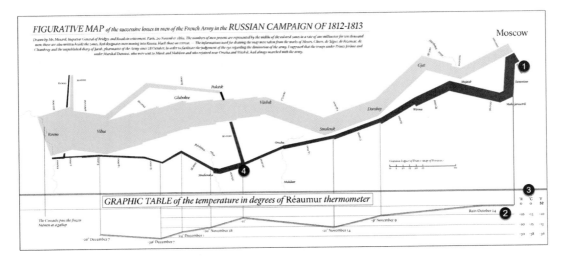

FIGURE 8.6 Focus on the retreat (the black lines).

While the positioning of the black line suggests otherwise, the retreat did not happen on a path that was south of the march to Moscow. Apparently, Minard thought the chart would be easier to read if he separated the paths. Also, the way the path toward Moscow is drawn, you might think all 422,000 lined up side by side. The black line gets thicker at (4) because the troops that had gone north to Polotsk returned to join the fighting as the French retreated.

In Minard's original version, the temperature was presented using only the Réaumur scale (0 = freezing, 80 = boiling). The English-language rendering also adds Fahrenheit and Celsius (Figure 8.7).

The *highest* temperature recorded during the retreat was freezing, making exposure the greatest cause of death during the withdrawal.

The retreat concludes in December. Napoleon started with 422,000 troops and ended with 10,000.

Imagine the Requirements

I look at any historical chart through a modern-day prism. What if corporate management foisted a requirements document on Minard? What would that have looked like?

- Show on a map where the campaign started and ended.

- Show where the troops traveled.

- Show how many troops were alive at key points in the journey.

- Make it clear which line depicts the onslaught and which depicts the retreat.

- The weather was a big factor during the retreat; make sure to show the temperature during key parts of the return.

- When you highlight those key parts, we need to know the date, too.

- This all needs to fit on one screen. In fact, it must fit on an iPad.

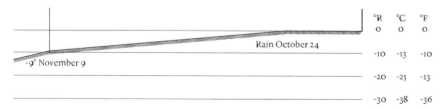

FIGURE 8.7 Plotting the temperature during the retreat. Minard annotates certain dates, and the height of the line reflects the temperature on those dates.

So is this the greatest chart of all time?

We'll come back to that in a moment, but first, I want to explore another chart that's shown in countless classes and seminars on data visualization.

THE NIGHTINGALE "ROSE" CHART

Florence Nightingale, the founder of modern nursing, was a polymath with formidable expertise in statistical analysis and visualization.

Her collection of three *rose* charts (she used the term *wedges*) showed the impact of changing sanitary conditions at the Scutari hospital in Turkey during the Crimean War in the mid-nineteenth century (Figure 8.8). Collaborating with hygiene expert William Farr, they determined that a soldier who made it to the hospital was more likely to die from cholera, typhus, and dysentery than from the wound he received on the battlefield.*

The three charts changed the British healthcare system.

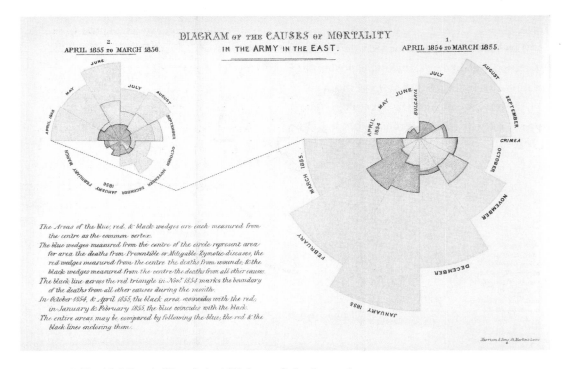

FIGURE 8.8 The Nightingale "Rose" chart (WellcomeCollection.org).

---

* Sadly, the risk of infection from hospital-associated infections is still a problem. According to health.gov, at any given time, about 1 in 25 inpatients have an infection related to hospital care. These infections lead to tens of thousands of deaths in the United States.

Interpreting the chart is far from obvious and I, like so many others who had to be taught how to interpret it, thought, "Why not show this as a bar chart?"

Here's what two of my data visualization colleagues think. According to RJ Andrews, who wrote about this in his essay "Florence Nightingale Is a Design Hero," "Critics suggest that [Nightingale's] mortality data is better shown in something more straightforward like a bar chart. But this is not true: Florence Nightingale made lots of bar charts. No one cares about them! Her roses gripped 1858 readers and they still hold our attention today."

In his book *How Charts Lie*, Alberto Cairo explains, "I believe [Nightingale's] goal wasn't just to inform but also to persuade with an intriguing, unusual, beautiful picture. A bar graph conveys the same message effectively, but it may not be as attractive to the eye."

> For a discussion on the chart, as well as an alternative rendering, see Jeffrey Shaffer's essay at bigpic.me/nightingale.

SOME SECOND OPINIONS

Imagine you are a seminar attendee, and you've just spent a full day listening to an admired expert proclaim the importance of the Minard and Nightingale charts. You may leave the seminar thinking, "This person told me that these are two of the best charts ever made. I guess we should be making charts like these in our organization."

Before we discuss whether or not that's a good idea, let's get two second opinions of the Minard Russian Campaign visualization. In a presentation he gave in 2006, marketing expert and author Seth Godin* said:

> I think this is one of the worst graphs ever made.
>
> He's [Tufte's] very happy because it shows five different pieces of information on three axes, and if you study it for 15 minutes, it really is worth 1,000 words.
>
> I don't think that is what graphs are for. I think you are trying to make a point in two seconds for people who are too lazy to read the forty words underneath.

In further correspondence I had with Godin, he writes: "Have you shown his chart to five smart people and had them 'grok' the idea? In the 21st century, I just don't believe that's how humans work."

Here's what Stephen Kosslyn, former chair of the Department of Psychology at Harvard University, writes in his book *Clear and to the Point: 8 Psychological Principles for Compelling PowerPoint Presentations*:

---

* A bow of appreciation to my fellow author of *The Big Book of Dashboards*, Jeffrey Shaffer, who first alerted me that not everyone thinks the Minard chart is the bees knees.

The display has never captivated me for the simple reason—given human processing limitations—I needed several minutes to figure it out. I didn't realize initially that five different variables are being shown simultaneously (which violates the Principle of Capacity Limitations) . . . I agree that M. Minard was amazingly clever and managed to cram a huge amount of information into a single display, but I can't agree that this is an effective way to communicate.

So how might someone remake the chart for a twenty-first-century audience?

Jorge Camões, data visualization consultant, trainer, and author of *Data at Work*, suggests something like Figure 8.9.

Yes, this approach is clearly a tongue-in-cheek rendering, but there is something to be said for the one, immediate, and clear takeaway: a great many men died.*

NAPOLEON'S RUSSIAN CAMPAIGN

Died
98%

Survived
2%

FIGURE 8.9 Jorge Camões's take on the famous Minard chart (Jorge Camões).

* There have been many modern retellings of the Minard chart. See bigpic.me/minard for some examples.

The goal of using data visualization to make better and faster decisions may lead people to think that any data visualization that is not immediately understood is a failure. Yes, a good visualization should allow you to see things that you might have missed, and to glean insights faster, but you still have to think. Elijah Meeks, cofounder of the Data Visualization Society, argues that there is a place for both fast and slow data visualization, and that we may be depriving our audiences of a rich, immersive understanding if we focus only on the fast.

Kendall Crolius, president of G100 Next Generation Leadership, is a big fan of the Minard chart because, once decoded, it conveys an amazing amount of information and insight. She asserts that a primary way companies benefit from graphicacy is that, once you build a dashboard and everyone knows how to read it, leaders can refer to it every day, week, or month to monitor the business. The big payoff is the recurring use of a familiar format.

Going back to the *Night Gallery* analogy, some people think the Minard chart is one of the greatest charts ever and others believe it is too confusing.

What should you do?

That is the crux of what data visualization in your organization is all about, and you will only be able to answer that if you consider the questions I brought up at the beginning of the book and in Chapter 6:

- Who is your audience?

- What is important to them?

- What do you want to tell them?

- How can you provide the greatest degree of understanding with the least amount of effort?*

The Minard and Nightingale visualizations worked during their time because both authors knew their audiences and knew them well. Minard was composing for a sophisticated, well-educated, mid-nineteenth-century audience. Minard knew readers of his charts, armed with rulers in hand† to accurately compare the size legend with lines or bars, would take a careful, thoughtful approach to studying the chart.

Rulers in hand! Can you imagine a busy executive seeing the Nightingale chart and

---

* As I stated earlier, the least amount of effort *for the audience*; the developers may have to put in a lot of effort.

† I highly recommend Sandra Rendgen's excellent book *The Minard System*. She describes the intended audience and explores many interesting and innovative charts (not just the famous Russian campaign), many of which are applicable to business scenarios today.

exclaiming, "This looks amazing! Let me get my protractor, so I can study this carefully!"

If Minard were alive today, would he make the same chart? Who would his audience be, and what would he want to tell them?

When he created the chart in 1869, at the age of 88, some 18 years after retiring from a successful career as a civil engineer, what was

he trying to impart? It's critical to note that Minard paired the Russian Campaign with another chart showing the massive losses of soldiers during Hannibal's 218 BC march over the Alps toward Rome (Figure 8.10). Hannibal lost 72 percent of his troops during the campaign.

Some argue that Minard's chart pairing constitutes an antiwar protest. Minard's obituary,

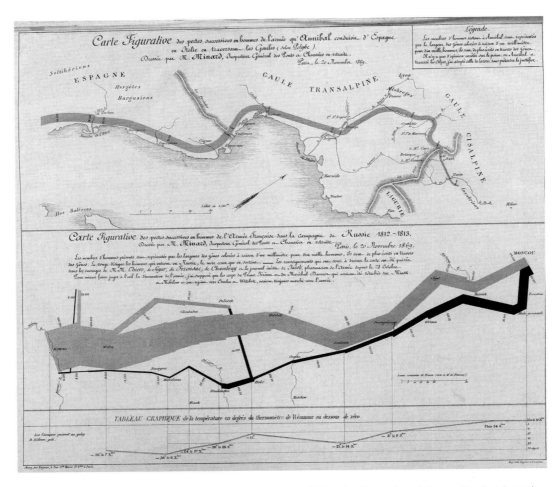

FIGURE 8.10 Hannibal's March over the Alps and Napoleon's Russian Campaign. (Minard, Charles-Joseph [1781–1870], "Tableaux graphiques et cartes figuratives," Bibliothèque numérique patrimoniale des ponts et chaussées, https://patrimoine.enpc.fr/document/ENPC01_Fol_10975.)

written by his son-in-law in 1871, the year after Minard's death, states: "Hannibal's army was thus reduced from 96,000 men to 26,000, and our great army of 422,000 combatants to only 10,000. The appearance is striking; and, especially today, it inspires bitter reflections on the cost to humanity of the follies of the conquerors and the pitiless thirst for military glory."*

So if Minard were alive today and wanted to effectively convey the cost of war to humanity, I can't help but think that he would take a different approach. Perhaps an animation similar to what Neil Halloran created to visualize and explain the loss of life during World War II (Figure 8.11). It's well worth watching.

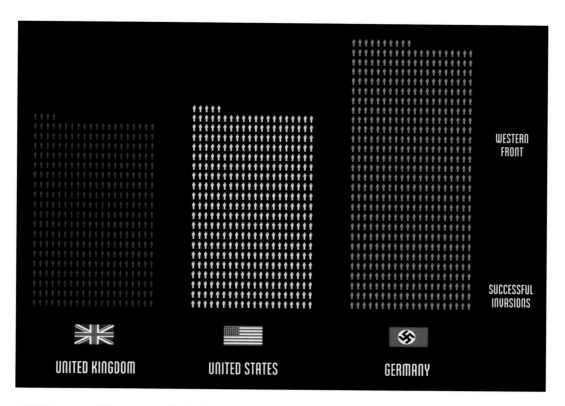

FIGURE 8.11 A still image from Neil Halloran's animated documentary *The Fallen of World War II* (Neil Halloran, http://fallen.io).

---

* See Victorin Chevallier, "Notice nécrologique sur M. Minard, inspecteur général des ponts et chaussées, en retraite," *Annales des ponts et chaussées : Mémoires et documents relatifs à l'art des constructions et au service de l'ingénieur,*" 1871, https://fr.wikisource.org/wiki/Notice_nécrologique_sur_M._Minard,_inspecteur_général_des_ponts_et_chaussées,_en _retraite.

We will never know what Minard would have done today, but I will argue that for your organization to succeed, the people creating charts and dashboards must understand the needs of those consuming the charts and dashboards.

Not addressing those needs is why I think so many books and seminars fail when they show the Russian Campaign and the Nightingale wedge chart. The writers and seminar leaders have not connected the dots between these charts and how people would use them in their organizations.

FLOW MAPS

Let's reconsider the Minard chart. The main element is the thick tan line showing forward movement and the thinner black line representing the retreat. This is a flow map, and it is a great way to show where things started, where things went, and how much went where. But it's presented in the context of an early nineteenth-century battle. Would you ever need a chart like this in modern business?

There are many cases in which a flow map is useful, but it can be hard to imagine its utility if you've only seen one in the context of a military campaign from over 200 years ago.

I do know of one case in which not only was a flow map useful, it completely changed the way an organization thought about its revenue streams.

We will see this example and several others in the next chapter.

CHAPTER 9

HOW YOU CAN CHANGE YOUR ORGANIZATION WITH DATA VISUALIZATION

want to share some real-world examples that people employed to change the way their organizations did business.

In some of these examples, an audience would see the visualizations only once, but that would be enough to help them make an informed decision. Other examples are used daily and are critical in helping organizations monitor performance and decide what should be prioritized. Some are instant reads, while others require teaching the audience how to read and interpret complicated dashboards. All have one thing in common: helping the intended audience see the big picture and make better decisions, faster.

My hope is you will look at these examples and think, "Yes! I see and understand this!" and "Yes, our organization can do this, too!"

DAILY ECOMMERCE REPORT

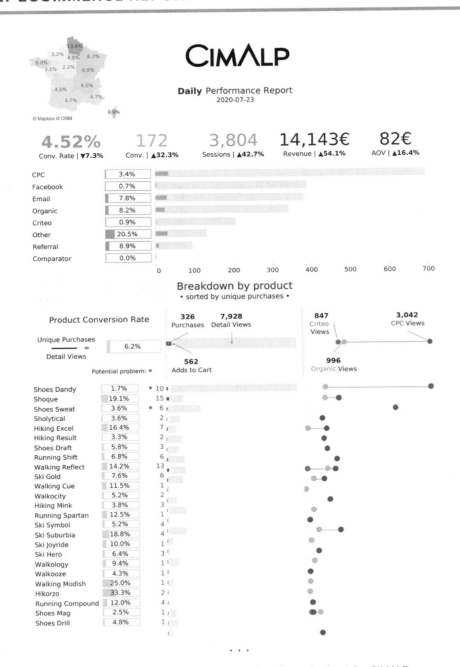

CIMALP

Daily Performance Report
2020-07-23

4.52%	**172**	**3,804**	**14,143€**	**82€**
Conv. Rate | ▼7.3%	Conv. | ▲32.3%	Sessions | ▲42.7%	Revenue | ▲54.1%	AOV | ▲16.4%

CPC	3.4%
Facebook	0.7%
Email	7.8%
Organic	8.2%
Criteo	0.9%
Other	20.5%
Referral	8.9%
Comparator	0.0%

Breakdown by product
• sorted by unique purchases •

Product Conversion Rate

Unique Purchases
————————— = 6.2%
Detail Views

	326	7,928		847	3,042
	Purchases	Detail Views		Criteo Views	CPC Views
		562		996	
		Adds to Cart		Organic Views	

Potential problem: ●

Product	Conv.	
Shoes Dandy	1.7%	10
Shoque	19.1%	15
Shoes Sweat	3.6%	6
Sholytical	3.6%	2
Hiking Excel	16.4%	7
Hiking Result	3.3%	2
Shoes Draft	5.8%	3
Running Shift	6.8%	6
Walking Reflect	14.2%	13
Ski Gold	7.6%	6
Walking Cue	11.5%	1
Walkocity	5.2%	2
Hiking Mink	3.8%	3
Running Spartan	12.5%	1
Ski Symbol	5.2%	4
Ski Suburbia	18.8%	4
Ski Joyride	10.0%	1
Ski Hero	6.4%	3
Walkology	9.4%	1
Walkooze	4.3%	1
Walking Modish	25.0%	1
Hikorzo	33.3%	2
Running Compound	12.0%	4
Shoes Mag	2.5%	1
Shoes Drill	4.8%	1

• • •

Designer: Dorian Banutoiu   Organization: Canonicalized, for CIMALP

Background

CIMALP is a French manufacturer that designs technical outdoor clothing, dedicated to the demanding practice of mountain sports.

The eCommerce division of the company needed a way to monitor daily click-to-purchase activity for every product it offers on its website.

The most important performance indicator is conversion rate (the number of transactions divided by views or visits). The second most important performance indicator is how much they spend on advertising.

Having a way to put conversion rate and paid-for traffic in the same view would do wonders for the organization because they would no longer have to spend hours checking individual product performance and they could avoid spending advertising funds on low-performing products.

The Original Version

Figure 9.1 shows the built-in report from the web analytics tool.

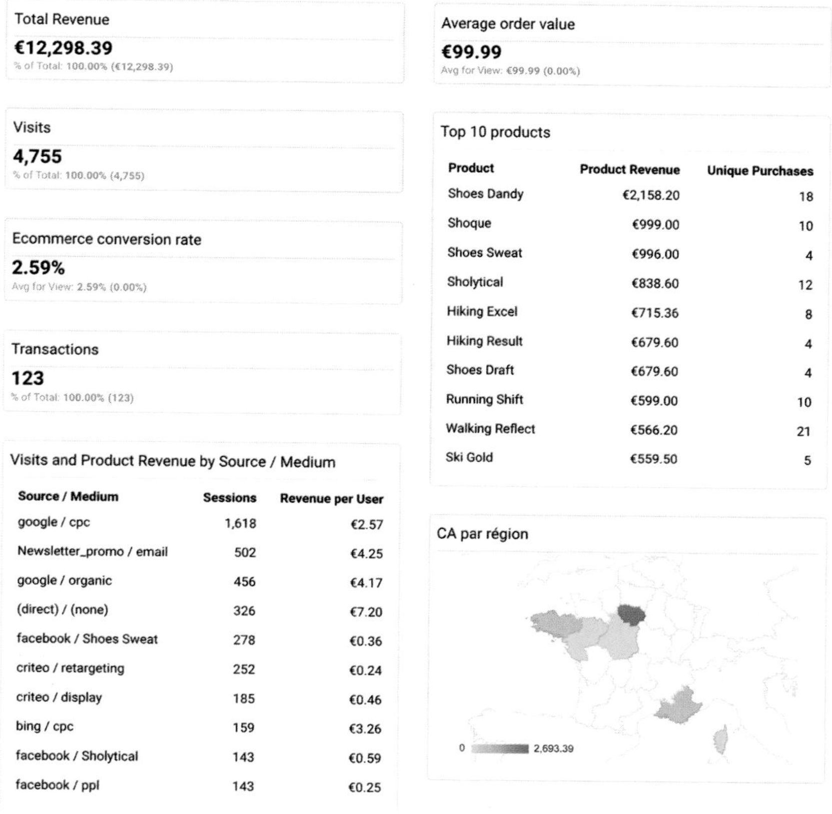

Total Revenue		
€12,298.39		
% of Total: 100.00% (€12,298.39)		

Average order value		
€99.99		
Avg for View: €99.99 (0.00%)		

Visits		
4,755		
% of Total: 100.00% (4,755)		

Top 10 products

Product	Product Revenue	Unique Purchases
Shoes Dandy	€2,158.20	18
Shoque	€999.00	10
Shoes Sweat	€996.00	4
Sholytical	€838.60	12
Hiking Excel	€715.36	8
Hiking Result	€679.60	4
Shoes Draft	€679.60	4
Running Shift	€599.00	10
Walking Reflect	€566.20	21
Ski Gold	€559.50	5

Ecommerce conversion rate		
2.59%		
Avg for View: 2.59% (0.00%)		

Transactions		
123		
% of Total: 100.00% (123)		

Visits and Product Revenue by Source / Medium

Source / Medium	Sessions	Revenue per User
google / cpc	1,618	€2.57
Newsletter_promo / email	502	€4.25
google / organic	456	€4.17
(direct) / (none)	326	€7.20
facebook / Shoes Sweat	278	€0.36
criteo / retargeting	252	€0.24
criteo / display	185	€0.46
bing / cpc	159	€3.26
facebook / Sholytical	143	€0.59
facebook / ppl	143	€0.25

CA par région

0   2,693.39

FIGURE 9.1 The original attempt to show conversion rates and advertising costs per product (Dorian Banutoiu, Canonicalized).

While nicely formatted, these metrics from the built-in web reporting application didn't do anything to help the organization quickly see what was performing well and what was performing poorly.

The Improved Version

Canonicalized, a data visualization consultancy, addressed all the shortcomings of the built-in report. In Figure 9.2 we see the top portion of the online dashboard.

The key performance indicators (also called *big-ass numbers*, or *BANs*), at the top (1, 2, and 3)

show both key metrics and serve as a color legend. They let us know that teal represents conversion rate (4.52%), light red represents conversions (172), and light gray represents the total number of sessions (3,804).

We can now apply these colors to the bar chart directly underneath the BANs. This combination of a regular and a 100% bar chart shows us the number of paid-for clicks, also known as cost-per-clicks or CPCs (4), the number of conversions (5), and the conversion rate (6).

Contrast this with the number of sessions and conversions for email (7) and its conversion rate (8).

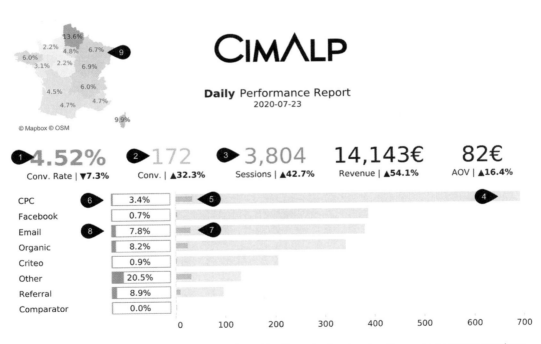

FIGURE 9.2 The top portion of the report designed by Canonicalized makes it easy to compare sessions and conversions.

The least important element is the map (9), but it has proven useful to spot issues by region, especially because sales are sensitive to weather changes.

As useful as the top part of the dashboard is, it's the bottom part that allows management to spot problems and fix them quickly (Figure 9.3).

There are three views for each product and a very well-rendered legend that explains them all. First, we see product conversion rate as a thermometer chart, allowing us to compare how filled up the bar is for each product (1).

The bar-in-bar-in-bar chart (2) allows the stakeholders to see views (gray), additions to cart (white), and purchases (black).

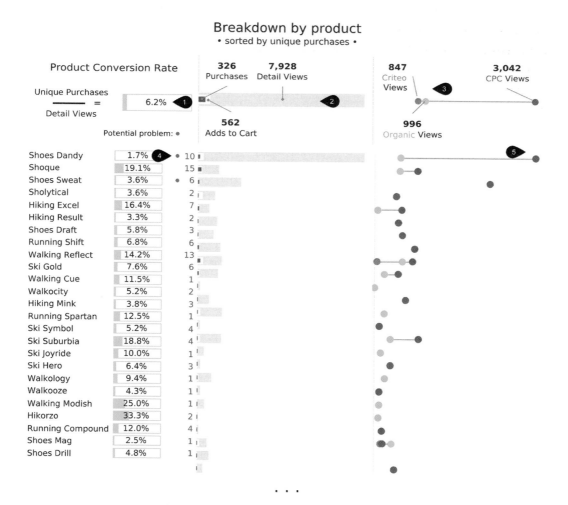

FIGURE 9.3 The bottom portion of the report makes it easy to compare performance for individual products (Canonicalized).

The color combination and size of the separate bars in the bar-in-bar-in-bar chart allow us to compare three key components (views, cart additions, and purchases) within a very compact area.

On the right (3), we see where the traffic is coming from (organic views, the paid service Criteo, or CPCs).

The indicator dot (4) reveals problems at a glance, drawing attention to product categories where there are very high costs per click (5) but few conversions. Are they low on stock of the product? Maybe there's not as much interest in the product this time of year? The person viewing the online report would need to do some further investigation, but in the previous version of the report, there was no way to determine that there was even a problem.

Either way, viewers can see immediately where they are spending a lot, where they are getting a good return, and where they are not.

The Impact

This is a complicated dashboard, and Dorian Banutoiu probably had to spend some time teaching his stakeholders how to use it and interpret the interrelated charts. That was a small investment. This report has completely changed the way this company runs its eCommerce business. The CEO, head of operations, and head of marketing review it every morning and never make a decision without reviewing this first.

Banutoiu has very elegantly solved many presentation challenges, such as how do you show views, adds to cart, and actual purchases across multiple products? The bar-in-bar-in-bar works perfectly.

Banutoiu also tackled the issue of showing rates/percentages versus actual amounts. This is a common issue and one that I think anyone reading this book will come across. Let me provide an example.

In our dashboard workshops, Jeffrey Shaffer, Andy Cotgreave, and I ask people how they would present the data shown in Figure 9.4.

Percentage of Goal

North	95%
South	105%
East	65%
West	135%

FIGURE 9.4 Percentage of goals reached for four regions.

After a brief discussion, the attendees propose something like the bar with reference line approach shown in Figure 9.5.

Attendees like this because we can see what is ahead of goal, what is behind goal, and by how much.

Without fail, attendees will point out this shortcoming: we don't know what the goals are for each region. That big miss in the East, was the goal $50,000 or $5 million?

This is a very valid point. Look at what happens when we include those numbers (Figure 9.6).

Well, that's a relief! The big miss in the East has only a modest impact on overall sales because the goal is much smaller.

How does Banutoiu address this? Does he show the actuals or the percentages?

He shows both (Figure 9.7).

This dashboard addresses many very common business use cases, and I suspect your organization will find a great number of applications for the techniques shown here.

Percentage of Goal

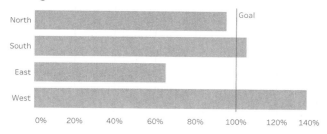

FIGURE 9.5 Percentage of goals reached using bars and a reference line.

Actual Versus Goal (|)

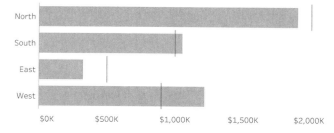

FIGURE 9.6 Showing actuals versus percentages presents a very different story.

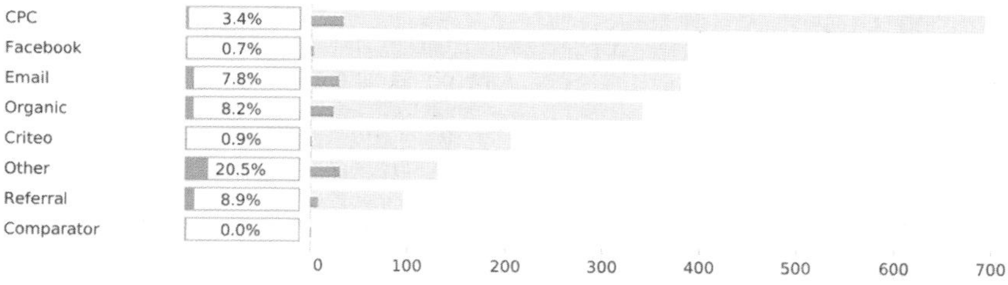

CPC	3.4%	
Facebook	0.7%	
Email	7.8%	
Organic	8.2%	
Criteo	0.9%	
Other	20.5%	
Referral	8.9%	
Comparator	0.0%	

FIGURE 9.7 Showing percentages and actuals side by side (Canonicalized).

UNDERSTANDING RACIAL AND ETHNIC DISPARITIES

Working to Reflect the Diverse Community We Serve

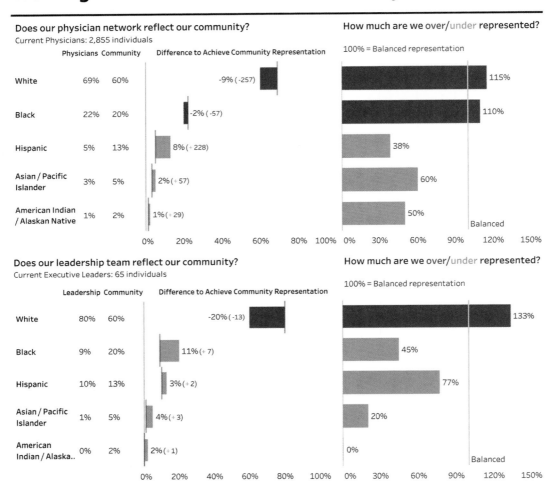

Designer: Lindsay Betzendahl   Organization: HealthDataViz

Background

An integrated healthcare organization, comprising physician practices, hospitals, and outpatient clinics, needed to highlight the organization's racial and ethnic diversity, or lack thereof. Their Diversity and Inclusion Executive Council built a visualization to show imbalances between the organization's workforce and the community it served. The overarching goal was to make sure those coming to the healthcare organization felt represented in both physician and leadership positions.

The Original Version

Figure 9.8 shows their first attempt at presenting imbalances.

Organization Workforce Racial/Ethnic Representation

Does our physician network reflect our community?

Race/Ethnicity	Community	Organization	Closing the Gap
White	1️⃣ 60%	69%	2️⃣ Reflects Community
Black	20%	22%	Reflects Community
Hispanic	3️⃣ 13%	5%	4️⃣ ▼
Asian / Pacific Islander	5%	3%	▼
American Indian / Alaskan Native	2%	1%	▼

Does our leadership reflect our community?

Race/Ethnicity	Community	Organization	Closing the Gap
White	60%	80%	Reflects Community
Black	20%	9%	▼
Hispanic	13%	10%	▼
Asian / Pacific Islander	5%	1%	▼
American Indian / Alaskan Native	2%	0%	▼

FIGURE 9.8 Original attempt to show disparity between the community and the healthcare organization that serves it (HealthDataViz).

Consider the percentage of people in the community and in the workforce that are White (1). The Closing the Gap column (2) indicates that the organization value reflects the community, when in fact White people are *overrepresented* (69 percent versus 60 percent).

Also consider the gap between Hispanics in the community and those in the organization (3). That is a very large gap but there's only a red arrow pointing down to indicate there is a problem (4). This is the drawback of just having arrows that point up or down; you can see there is an issue, but you then have to look at the numbers to determine if the gap is big or if it is small.

You are asking a lot of your audience when you do this.

The Improved Version

HealthDataViz's makeover in Figure 9.9 addresses both shortcomings of the original version.

Consider (1) where the blue bar is anchored at 69 percent and moves left until it reaches a value of 60 percent. This indicates that there should be a reduction of 9 points, or 257 people. Another way to express this is to say that White people are at 115 percent of the representation

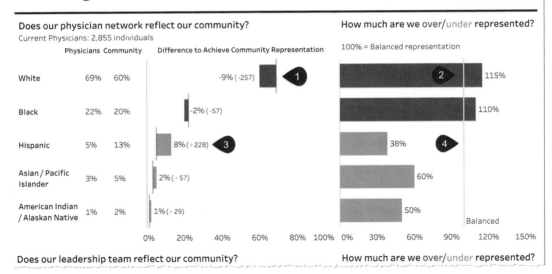

FIGURE 9.9 Updated visualization in which it is much easier to see where populations are over- and underrepresented and by how much (HealthDataViz).

goal (2), indicating clearly the overrepresentation of this population in the organization compared to the community. An equal representation would be 100 percent. Contrast that with Hispanics where the bar starts at 5 percent and moves to the *right* until it reaches 13 percent, indicating an 8-point gap and a need to increase staff by 228 people to be an accurate reflection of the community (3). Another way to express this is that the organization is 38 percent toward a goal of accurate representation (4).

The Impact

These visualizations helped the organization identify where they needed to focus, how near or far they were to closing the gap in racial/ethnic representation, and the exact numbers they needed to achieve that. Effective business execution is about focus and setting priorities. This dashboard will help management do that.

A Word of Caution

No one is suggesting that the organization immediately lay off 257 White people and 57 Black people and hire 228 Hispanics, 57 Asians/Pacific Islanders, and 29 American Indians/Alaskan Natives. Rather, the organization now has a much clearer sense of where the imbalances are and how, moving forward, to address them.

With time, it would be great to see longitudinal data added to the dashboard so the organization can see the strides it has made.

REIMAGINING PHARMACEUTICAL STUDY RESULTS FOR TWO AUDIENCES

Let's understand Serentiva preference

Of the 99 patients in our study,

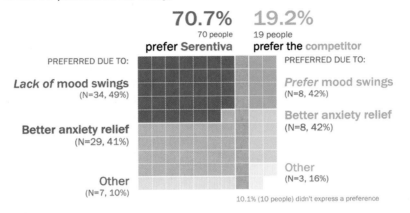

70.7%
70 people
prefer Serentiva

19.2%
19 people
prefer the competitor

PREFERRED DUE TO:

Lack of mood swings
(N=34, 49%)

Better anxiety relief
(N=29, 41%)

Other
(N=7, 10%)

PREFERRED DUE TO:

Prefer mood swings
(N=8, 42%)

Better anxiety relief
(N=8, 42%)

Other
(N=3, 16%)

10.1% (10 people) didn't express a preference

UnaVersa

LACK OF MOOD SWINGS & ANXIETY RELIEF DRIVE SERENTIVA PREFERENCE

Of the 99 patients in our study,

70.7%
expressed preference for
Serentiva (N=70), mainly
due to **lack of mood swings**
and **better anxiety relief**

19.2%
expressed preference for
the competitor (N=19)*,
citing better anxiety relief
and preference for mood
swings as primary reasons.

Reasons for preference
■ Prefer Serentiva
■ Prefer competitor

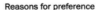
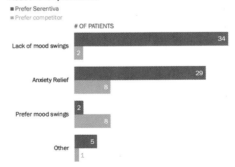

OF PATIENTS

Lack of mood swings — 34 / 2

Anxiety Relief — 29 / 8

Prefer mood swings — 2 / 8

Other — 5 / 1

UnaVersa

Designer: Cole Nussbaumer Knaflic   Organization: storytelling with data

Background

The following is a real scenario, with names and details changed to preserve confidentiality.

The pharmaceutical company UnaVersa concluded a marketing study comparing their recently FDA-approved anti-anxiety drug, Serentiva, to their primary competitor's. The study included patient participants who had taken both Serentiva and the competitor product for a set period of time. The results showed a marked preference for Serentiva versus the competition.

The study results were then shared with two primary audiences as part of overall marketing efforts. The first audience was a group of psychiatrists who regularly speak at industry events. The second audience was UnaVersa's own sales representatives, who call on doctors to increase awareness of their products. In both cases, the goal was to equip the given audience with an understanding of the study results and educational talking points that they could share with their respective audiences—physicians writing anti-anxiety prescriptions—in the hope that they would write more Serentiva prescriptions.

The Original Version

The team had some great data to share, specifically:

- A significant preference for Serentiva over the competitor's product.

- What the vast majority preferred about Serentiva.

- What the small minority liked about the competition.

Figure 9.10 shows the single-slide summary that was initially used to communicate the findings.

Goodness, talk about burying the lede! The key takeaway—that 70.7 percent of survey participants preferred Serentiva versus 19.2 percent for the competitor—is sitting in the bottom-left corner, and it doesn't even have a pink rounded rectangle around it like the other, less significant findings do!

Needless to say, the analytics team that created the slide was finding it difficult to get their intended message across. They found that people frequently misinterpreted the graphs, and some even concluded that more people experienced anxiety relief with the competitor's product!

The organization hired Cole Nussbaumer Knaflic, the founder of the company storytelling with data, to work with the team to better understand the needs of the audience and to communicate Serentiva's advantages.

One thing that became clear quickly was that there were two very different audiences, and that the team would need to develop two very different approaches to reach them.

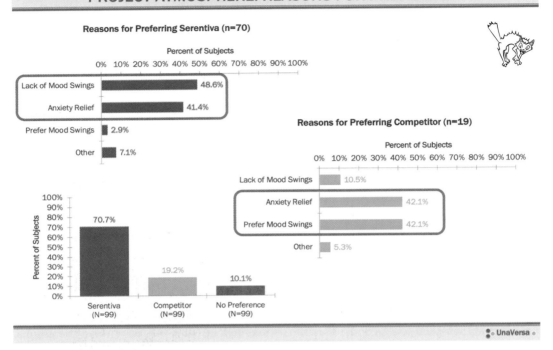

FIGURE 9.10 Original visualization that tried to show the preferences for Serentiva versus a competitor (storytelling with data).

Audience 1

WHO: Psychiatrist speakers

WHAT: Influence peers to prescribe Serentiva

HOW: Live presentation (generally over lunch or dinner, competing for attention with food, table conversations, and networking)

Audience 2

WHO: UnaVersa salespeople

WHAT: Influence doctors to prescribe Serentiva

HOW: Visit to a doctor's office, with a detail piece (static handout; competing against the clock)

After getting shared clarity on these two audiences, Cole and the team turned back to the data. The numbers were relatively simple once they put the main takeaways into words. They brainstormed different visuals that could work and took turns drawing on the whiteboard, applying many of the techniques we discussed in Chapter 6. In this manner, they were able to quickly iterate, sketching a number of ideas and discussing the pros and cons of each. At the end of the working session, they had two concrete ideas to realize.

The Improved Version for Audience 1

Cole and the team decided to go with a novel approach for the industry events. First, they wanted to reinforce the idea that the study wasn't made up of data; rather, it was composed of patients—people. This led them to visually encode each person individually (versus aggregating segments of patients into a single bar of data, for example). We saw how effective this can be in the jitterplot showing the incidence of diabetes in the Introduction. Second, they wanted something eye-catching to get people's attention. They thought that a less common visual would do this and work well in a live setting, where they could build it *piece by piece* so that, though unfamiliar, it would feel intuitive. As an added benefit, they thought the anticipation of what would come next—the introduction of a sense of intrigue—would help keep the psychiatrists' attention for the duration of the short presentation.

The following progression, starting with Figure 9.11, shows some of the resulting visuals they assembled for the presentation.

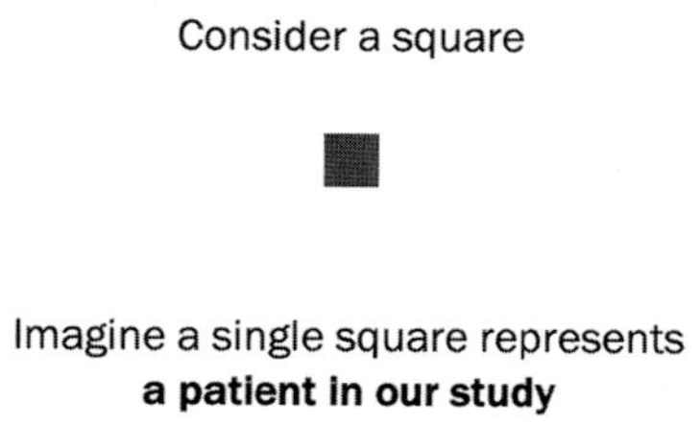

Consider a square

Imagine a single square represents
a patient in our study

FIGURE 9.11 The "seduction" begins. The presenter starts by explaining what a small square represents (storytelling with data).

Here's a waffle chart showing all of the survey respondents (Figure 9.12).

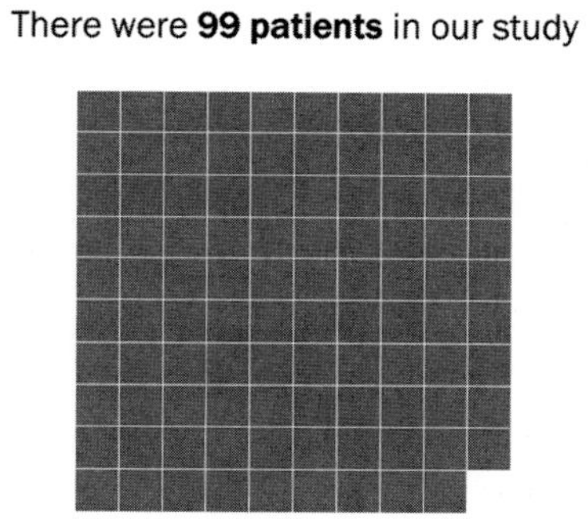

There were **99 patients** in our study

FIGURE 9.12 The narrative continues. The audience now sees the universe of respondents (storytelling with data).

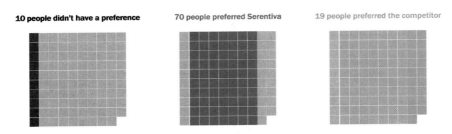

FIGURE 9.13 Respondents' preferences (storytelling with data).

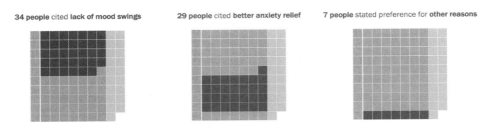

FIGURE 9.14 Reasons for preferring Serentiva (storytelling with data).

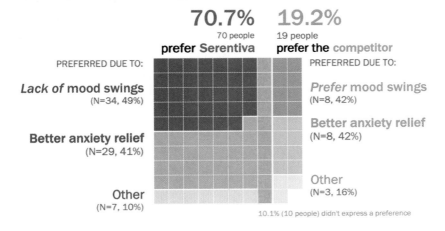

FIGURE 9.15 Final visualization showing that almost 71 percent of respondents preferred Serentiva, and their reasons (storytelling with data).

Survey participants were asked which anti-anxiety drug they preferred. Figure 9.13 shows the results (shown one image at a time).

Survey participants were then asked what drives their preferences. Figure 9.14 shows the reasons why those 70 people preferred Serentiva.

The dance continued and eventually the presenter showed the culminating slide (Figure 9.15).

Interestingly enough, of the 19 people who preferred the competitor, eight cited a preference *for* mood swings. Go figure!

Note that the presentation didn't consist of one visualization. Instead, it started with a single square and the presenter, acting as a guide, slowly added more and more layers. By the end of the narrative, the audience could see how all the pieces fit together and why so many more respondents preferred Serentiva.

While this slow unveiling worked well for the psychiatrists, it would not work for the time-crunched sales representatives. They needed to deliver the message, clearly, in one compact visual.

The Improved Version for Audience 2

When salespeople call on doctors' offices, the biggest constraint they face is time; physicians will typically spend a few minutes at most to hear their spiel. Given this, the team didn't want the salespeople to take any time talking about how to read a graph. By simplifying as much as possible and using a familiar graph type, the team could get the conversation more quickly centered on the study outcome and findings.

The original slide in Figure 9.10 achieved this to some degree using only bar charts. Part of the confusion in that initial version was that it included multiple graphs depicting various percentages. These were difficult to reconcile quickly and also made it easy for people to make bad comparisons. Cole and the team wanted to preserve the simplicity, but tie it all together in a way that was easy to interpret.

In the updated version, they put the primary takeaways into words. They turned the most important summary data points into simple numbers. And they included a single graph and focused it on the number of patients, so people could see the varying distribution across reasons for preference, but also the clear difference in scale between the preference for Serentiva and the competitor. Their final slide looked like Figure 9.16.

Look at those bars! Serentiva is way ahead on every front, except Prefer mood swings. Who prefers mood swings?

The Impact

They immediately noted an easier time helping their audiences understand the study: there were fewer oddball questions, and people were

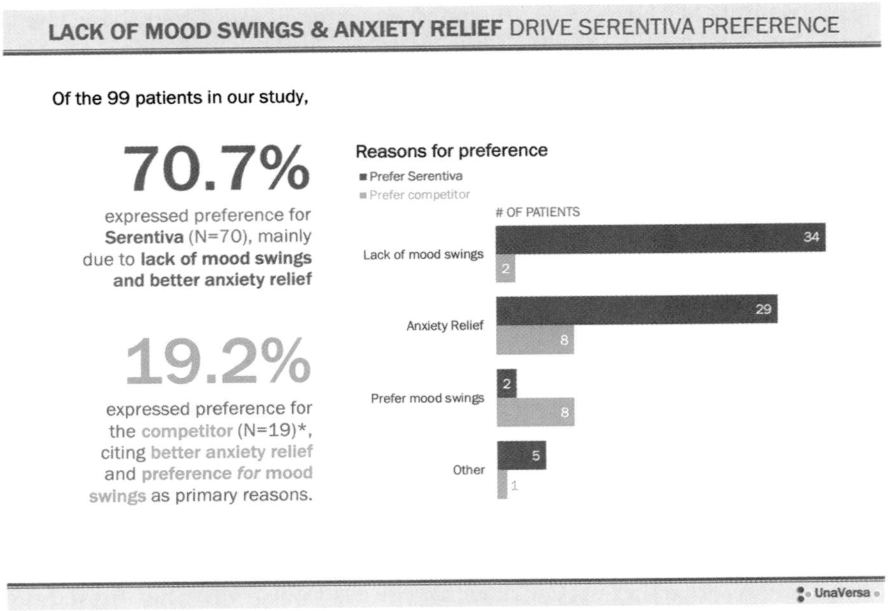

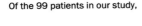

FIGURE 9.16 Single slide designed to educate the ever-so-busy physicians (storytelling with data).

more quickly able to grasp and articulate the key takeaways. When it came to success with the ultimate audiences, both the psychiatrist speakers and salespeople reported better questions and conversations when speaking about the study with their respective physician audiences. But perhaps a better indicator than any of this anecdotal evidence of success was the immediate increase in prescriptions UnaVersa noted for their new product.

By thoughtfully considering the various audiences and their needs—and designing communications with those top of mind—Cole and her client turned a confusing slide into two targeted resources that afforded understanding and drove action. Success!

Alternatives

This is a great example of the importance of knowing your audience, and in this case, audiences. When I first saw the waffle chart, I thought of Cotgreave's law: "The longer an innovative visualization exists, the probability someone says it should have been a line/bar chart approaches 1."

Indeed, I wanted to see the data rendered using a bar chart (Figure 9.17).

Yes, it's easier to make accurate comparisons, but there was something compelling about showing how each square represented a person. Maybe we could combine the two and make a unit bar chart (Figure 9.18)?

Of the 99 people surveyed, people preferred

FIGURE 9.17 "That should be a bar chart!" For certain, it's easier to make accurate comparisons with a bar chart.

Of the 99 people surveyed, people preferred

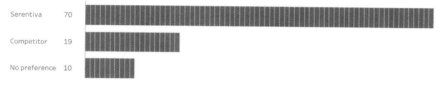

FIGURE 9.18 A unit bar chart.

With this, I can see the individual respondents and compare the overall length. But why stop there? What about using some gender-neutral icons and creating a pictogram (Figure 9.19)?

Yes, this works, but it looks cutesy, and that might not work for the intended audience.

Indeed, Cole and the team explored all of these options, and it was the rarely used waffle chart—with a guide to walk the audience through the steps, piquing interest, and showing how to solve the puzzle—that resonated with the intended audience.

And the one-pager with bar charts for the time-crunched salespeople? That worked, too.

Of the 99 people surveyed, people preferred

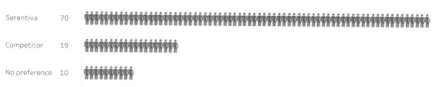

FIGURE 9.19 A pictogram.

INSIGHTS FROM A KPI DASHBOARD

Note: the data represented below is not real.

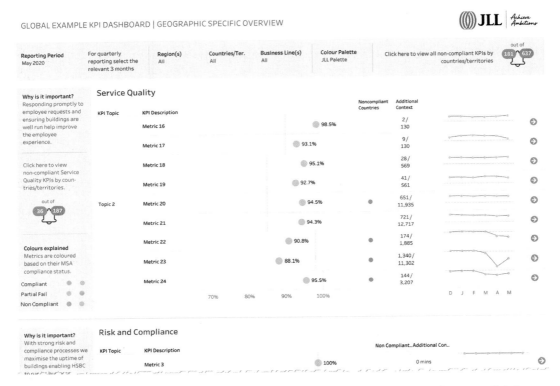

Designers: Hesham Eissa, with Simon Beaumont and Chris Lay   Organization: JLL Corporate Solutions

Background

JLL, a leader in facilities management, oversees a global portfolio of properties, ranging from 42-floor towers to small-town retail sites. Management needs to monitor key metrics and attend to anything that is underperforming.

The Original Version

Figure 9.20 shows the business intelligence team's initial attempt at presenting a key performance indicator (KPI) dashboard.

Here we see a highlight table that displays global performance across 30+ KPIs. The user

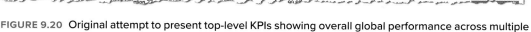

KPI GLOBAL DASHBOARD   Last Updated: 10.01.2020

KPI Date
December, 2019   Data updated 10th day of the month.   Global Drill Down
Global   Three Tier Analysis - Global,
Region, Country

	Global: Cost		
KPI Topic	KPI Description	KPI Target	
Metric 1	Description 2	< 100%	100.00%
Metric 2	Description 5	Full year increase over same period in previous year	PASS
	Description 6	Full year increase over same period in previous year	PASS
	Description 7	Full improvement in score	53.30%
Metric 3	Description 1	Green >= 100% Imp'd | Amber >= 100% w/F'cast | Red < 100% w/F'cast	104.28%
Metric 4	Description 3	Meet or exceed expected completion % each month	100.00%

	Global: Risk		
KPI Topic	KPI Description	KPI Target	
Metric 5	Description 13	>= 98%	99.82%
	Description 14	100%	99.09%
	Description 15	>= 98%	98.78%
	Description 18	>=99.995%	100%
	Description 19	>=99.995%	100%
	Description 20	>=99.95%	100%
	Description 21	>=99.9%	100%

FIGURE 9.20 Original attempt to present top-level KPIs showing overall global performance across multiple regions and 50 countries (JLL Corporate Solutions).

can apply a filter and explore the same KPIs by region or by country. The goal is to show where performance had been met or not met using traditional traffic light colors (red and green).

Assuming you are not among the roughly 1 out of 10 men or 1 out of 100 women globally who have red-green color vision deficiency, it's easy to see where things are going well (almost everywhere) and where things are performing poorly (that one red KPI). So what's not to love?

Consider the many things we cannot tell from this dashboard:

- The item in red: Did we miss by a lot or just a little? Did it just crop up this month, or has it been going on for a while?

- All those wonderful green KPIs: Did we crush the goals by a lot, or are there some that just squeaked through?

- Most importantly, while the organization may be doing well overall, are there regions, countries, cities, individual properties, and so on that were gross underperformers?

That last question is the biggest issue. Think of having a sales quota of $1 million for the company. You come in at $1.1 million, and everybody celebrates.

It turns out that one of the four regions of the company performed terribly, but the other three regions more than made up for it. Imagine how much better the overall performance would be if that one region had performed better?

A well-run organization needs to be able to see where there are shortcomings and attend to them quickly.

Beware of "Watermelons"

I first heard this expression from data visualization and BI expert Marc Reguera from Microsoft. It refers to a KPI that is green on the outside but red on the inside, meaning that the overall measure is okay (green), but there are pockets of trouble below the surface (red). This example and the one that follows both address the watermelon problem very effecively.

The Improved Version

Figure 9.21 shows the top portion of the improved version.

The warning bell at the top of the screen (1) indicates that there are 181 noncompliant metrics out of a total of 637. This is an aggregation of all metrics across all countries. A country can have more than one noncompliant metric.

The warning bell along the left (2) indicates there are 36 noncompliant countries/territories out of 187 for Service Quality. Scrolling down will show similar warning bells for different areas (e.g., Risk and Compliance, Workplace, Sustainability, etc.)

Let's explore some of the details of the inner portions of the dashboard and see what we can glean (Figure 9.22).

Throughout the dashboard we see that blue indicates where the organization is exceeding a target and orange indicates where it is below target. The dashboard has a toggle that allows

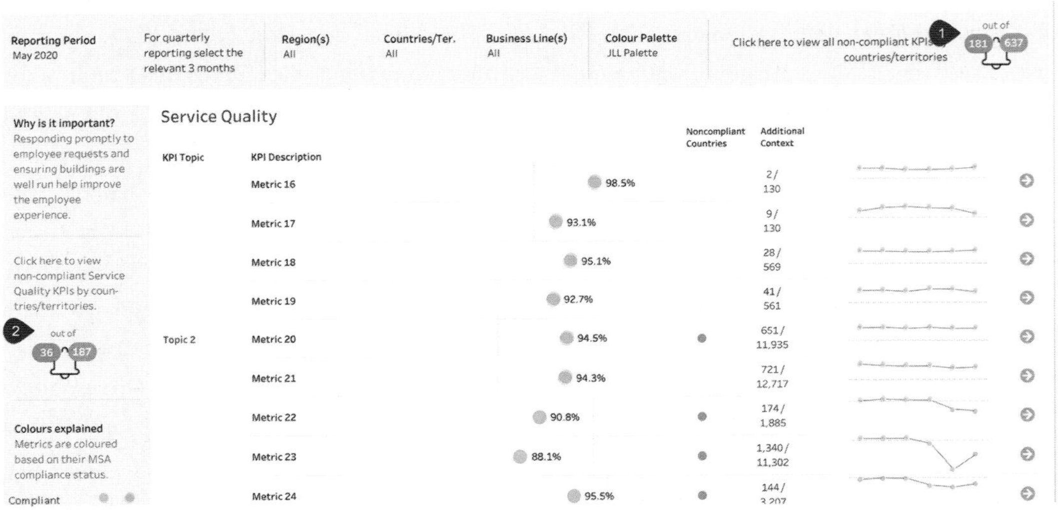

FIGURE 9.21 Top portion of dashboard showing overall and specific area warning bells (JLL Corporate Solutions).

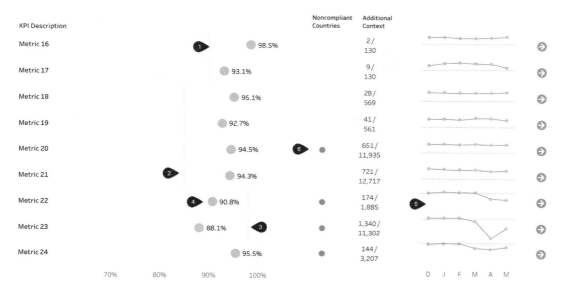

FIGURE 9.22 The meat of the dashboard (JLL Corporate Solutions).

people to use traditional red and green instead of blue and orange, if they prefer.

And just what are these targets?

If this were the actual dashboard, we could hover over the line (1) and see that Metrics 16 and 17 have a target of 90 percent. Metrics 18 through 21 have a target of 85 percent (2). Metrics 22 and 23 have a target of 95 percent. This explains why the dot for Metric 22 with 90.8 percent is orange (4).

One question that should come to mind is whether Metric 22 being below target is a new development or something that has gone on for a while. The miniature line charts, called *sparklines*, (5) show us that the last two months have been a problem (the two orange dots at the end of the line).

Orange dots (6) are used to show where there is an underlying noncompliant country for that metric.

Have a look at Metric 20. It shows 94.5 percent, which is well above the target of 85 percent. Why is there an orange dot (6) indicating there is a problem?

Hovering over the dot answers the question (Figure 9.23).

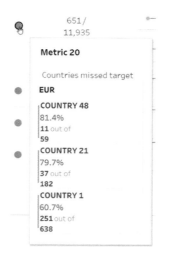

FIGURE 9.23
The power of little dots. Here, we can inspect the problem and see that three countries in Europe have missed their numbers (JLL Corporate Solutions).

This is the important finding that the first dashboard hides. While the organization as a whole is meeting its numbers, there are some countries that are not, and this allows the stakeholder to not only see that there is a problem (the dot), but to also be able to focus on the countries where the problem (or problems) can be found.

The column immediately to the right of the orange dots also provides insights into where shortcomings can be found (Figure 9.24).

The size of the bar indicates the number of failed elements. The color of the bar indicates whether an entire country is below goal (as we see with the orange bars for Countries 1, 21, and 48 in Region 1) or if the countries are meeting their goals, but some individual transactions within the country missed their targets (Region 2 and Region 3).

Finally, for each of the metrics there is an arrow that takes the audience to another dashboard to explore details (see the far-right column in Figure 9.22).

The Impact

This dashboard is an embodiment of what good data visualization is all about—quickly finding insights that would otherwise be hidden. It enables the user to see the big picture (i.e., that there are shortcomings), and allows them to drill down into the details of exactly where those shortcomings are.

What used to take hours now takes minutes.

I asked the dashboard authors about both the orange dot and the additional context indicators (boxed, in Figure 9.25).

Why not make the dots and numbers something the audience can compare, like what we see in Figure 9.26?

The designers had certainly considered this, but knowing their audience, they believed it would be graphic overload, so they settled on the simple dot and text table, confident the stakeholders would hover to explore the details.

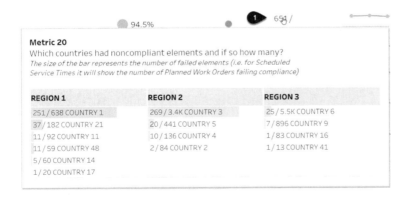

FIGURE 9.24 A quick glance at every place where Metric 20 is below goal (JLL Corporate Solutions).

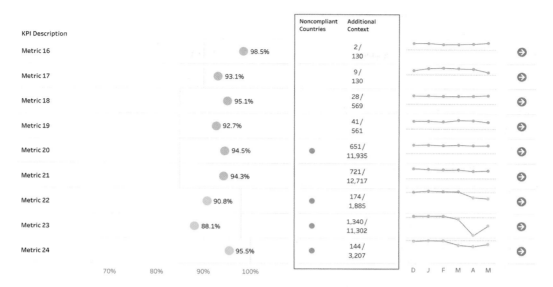

FIGURE 9.25 The orange dot indicates at least one country is not hitting its numbers. The numbers to the right indicate the number of noncompliant elements out of the total number of elements measured (JLL Corporate Solutions).

Noncompliant Countries	Additional Context
2	2
3	9
	28
1	41
3	651
1	721
7	174
16	1,340
7	144

FIGURE 9.26 Alternative approach to showing number of countries that are non-compliant and number of elements that are noncompliant (JLL Corporate Solutions).

A DIFFERENT APPROACH TO KPI DASHBOARDS

Note: the data represented below is not real.

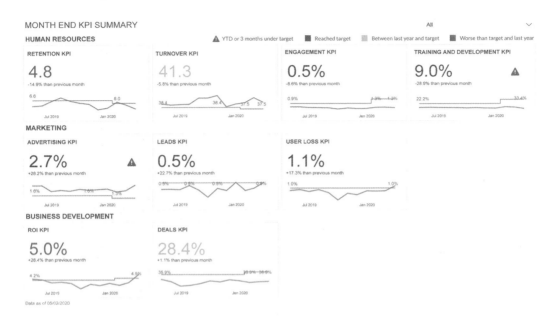

Designer: Nick Snapp   Organization: Voyant Data

Background

One of Voyant Data's clients needed to monitor KPIs on a massive scale (global, regional, and individual locations). They needed the ability to spot problems from a high level and drill down to the granular level with just a few clicks.

The Original Version

Figure 9.27 shows the organization's initial attempt at presenting a KPI dashboard.

Here we see a highlight table that displays global performance across hundreds of rows (only 50 or so are shown here). There's a lot of

Month End KPI Summary

Enterprise Wide Performance

Reached yearly target
Between baseline and target
Below baseline

Better than last month
Worse than last month

Lever	Metric	Region	Baseline	Target '20	3 Months Rolling Average	YTD	Apr-19	May-19	Jun-19	Jul-19	Aug-19	Sep-19	Oct-19	Nov-19	Dec-19	Jan-20	Feb-20	Mar-20
HR	Retention KPI	Total	16.8	15.6	5.9	6.3	17.1	15.9	15.2	16.8	15.0	15.2	15.3	15.6	15.6	13.9	15.0	14.4
		New York	12.8	13.1	4.9	5.2	13.8	12.4	11.4	12.8	11.7	13.7	12.8	13.1	15.6	11.5	13.1	11.4
		Texas	21.0	16.5	6.4	6.9	19.5	19.5	16.2	21.0	14.9	15.0	16.4	16.5	15.9	14.7	16.0	16.2
		Idaho	22.6	26.4	8.9	9.3	21.8	18.6	20.0	22.6	21.8	28.1	26.7	26.4	23.7	23.4	22.0	19.9
		California	18.5	15.2	5.5	6.1	15.0	15.7	15.0	18.5	15.8	15.7	15.2	15.2	13.9	13.8	13.7	13.3
		Georgia	18.3	13.0	6.8	6.6	18.7	17.0	17.2	18.3	14.8	13.6	16.8	13.0	15.8	17.4	14.8	17.6
		Washington	21.5	18.2	6.8	7.2	18.7	18.8	17.6	21.5	17.0	17.0	17.7	18.2	16.0	16.9	17.2	15.7
		Phoenix	13.7	15.1	5.7	5.9	16.9	14.6	13.0	13.7	16.9	13.6	13.0	15.1	15.7	12.3	15.3	14.4
		Oregon	18.8	15.5	5.8	6.2	16.3	16.3	15.0	18.8	14.4	14.3	14.7	15.5	13.4	13.4	15.1	14.5
		Vermont	18.3	17.3	6.4	7.1	20.4	16.9	18.6	18.3	18.0	17.4	17.7	17.3	17.2	14.5	15.9	16.4
		North Dakota	10.4	12.6	5.0	5.1	14.6	13.6	13.5	10.4	12.6	12.2	11.7	12.6	13.0	12.1	13.9	10.8
		Nevada	16.5	14.8	5.7	6.1	15.5	15.3	16.8	16.5	13.7	15.1	15.2	14.8	14.6	14.7	13.5	13.6
	Turnover KPI	Total	94.1	93.9	38.5	38.7	95.5	97.4	96.5	92.9	95.8	95.0	94.1	91.9	96.2	96.5	93.9	93.4
		New York	83.3	82.0	34.4	35.4	87.2	89.5	92.2	89.6	92.3	88.9	83.3	83.7	82.7	85.5	82.0	85.7
		Texas	80.2	88.8	36.2	33.6	77.8	75.8	82.3	72.5	94.7	81.9	80.2	76.6	82.1	90.4	88.8	87.1
		Idaho	121.6	114.7	47.2	49.0	123.9	129.1	118.4	114.1	125.2	127.5	121.6	116.0	121.0	118.3	114.7	114.5
		California	102.2	99.3	40.2	40.5	101.7	101.2	98.6	97.6	96.8	98.6	102.2	98.7	101.0	101.4	99.3	95.1
		Georgia	99.6	101.6	41.0	40.0	98.9	99.3	94.8	94.2	94.5	97.4	99.6	97.9	99.9	100.6	101.6	100.0
		Washington	93.3	91.8	38.3	38.5	94.2	95.5	96.5	92.9	93.9	92.4	93.3	92.5	100.2	102.5	91.8	88.1
		Phoenix	91.4	87.7	37.9	37.5	90.7	93.8	98.0	90.3	83.7	88.2	91.4	93.0	96.5	100.5	87.7	91.3
		Oregon	89.8	93.4	37.3	37.8	92.8	94.1	95.9	89.1	92.5	92.6	89.8	90.5	101.1	94.9	93.4	86.7
		Vermont	105.3	102.3	42.0	43.1	108.0	116.8	107.3	107.1	104.2	104.2	105.3	101.8	105.2	103.2	102.3	103.8
		North Dakota	90.9	85.8	36.6	37.3	98.9	98.7	92.4	92.0	88.0	93.7	90.9	87.0	87.8	90.5	85.8	93.7
		Nevada	96.5	94.8	38.2	38.7	97.5	97.2	95.8	97.1	94.1	95.7	96.5	91.7	94.7	92.1	94.8	94.5
	Engagement KPI	Total	0.39%	1.32%	0.45%	0.43%	2.42%	2.43%	2.44%	2.45%	2.41%	2.40%	2.37%	2.46%	2.45%	2.47%	2.43%	2.44%
		New York	0.84%	1.08%	0.93%	0.96%	2.98%	2.95%	3.05%	2.95%	3.02%	2.91%	2.85%	3.05%	2.97%	2.99%	2.89%	2.91%
		Texas	0.96%	1.34%	1.18%	0.97%	2.83%	2.76%	2.90%	2.87%	2.80%	2.78%	2.82%	3.13%	3.20%	3.20%	3.03%	3.30%
		Idaho	0.04%	0.94%	0.05%	0.05%	2.04%	2.04%	2.03%	2.06%	2.05%	2.06%	2.04%	2.05%	2.06%	2.04%	2.05%	2.05%
		California	0.05%	1.06%	0.08%	0.07%	2.03%	2.04%	2.07%	2.07%	2.09%	2.07%	2.07%	2.05%	2.07%	2.08%	2.09%	2.06%
		Georgia	0.33%	1.10%	0.21%	0.25%	2.43%	2.35%	2.28%	2.23%	2.23%	2.23%	2.15%	2.22%	2.24%	2.26%	2.19%	2.18%
		Washington	0.12%	1.74%	0.13%	0.09%	2.07%	2.05%	2.06%	2.15%	2.07%	2.04%	2.11%	2.07%	2.07%	2.10%	2.12%	2.17%
		Phoenix	0.20%	0.87%	0.26%	0.25%	2.26%	2.29%	2.25%	2.29%	2.23%	2.18%	2.19%	2.24%	2.24%	2.28%	2.31%	2.21%
		Oregon	0.14%	1.99%	0.20%	0.19%	2.14%	2.13%	2.16%	2.20%	2.20%	2.19%	2.18%	2.22%	2.22%	2.22%	2.20%	2.18%
		Vermont	0.15%	1.32%	0.16%	0.17%	2.09%	2.25%	2.13%	2.33%	2.12%	2.20%	2.14%	2.18%	2.11%	2.16%	2.16%	2.16%
		North Dakota	1.40%	1.42%	1.23%	1.45%	3.87%	3.63%	3.62%	3.54%	3.52%	3.46%	3.25%	3.35%	3.41%	3.36%	3.28%	3.06%
		Nevada	0.03%	1.27%	0.08%	0.07%	2.02%	2.05%	2.05%	2.06%	2.05%	2.05%	2.07%	2.10%	2.08%	2.08%	2.10%	2.07%
	Train and Dev KPI	Total	9.9%	33.4%	11.6%	10.7%	12.90%	12.59%	11.90%	12.12%	11.88%	11.79%	11.51%	12.92%	13.68%	13.62%	13.42%	13.84%
		New York	21.3%	27.6%	22.8%	22.9%	25.85%	25.85%	25.84%	23.60%	25.23%	22.67%	22.39%	26.21%	26.22%	25.80%	23.36%	25.23%
		Texas	25.5%	35.6%	31.5%	25.6%	24.98%	23.34%	25.31%	23.44%	22.45%	22.98%	23.73%	30.90%	33.72%	32.14%	31.98%	36.35%
		Idaho	1.2%	32.8%	1.5%	1.6%	3.55%	3.38%	3.01%	3.84%	3.81%	4.24%	3.47%	3.61%	4.08%	3.37%	3.40%	3.78%
		California	1.6%	33.7%	2.5%	2.0%	3.06%	3.27%	3.85%	3.74%	4.62%	4.13%	3.92%	3.43%	4.22%	4.44%	4.97%	3.96%
		Georgia	9.4%	31.0%	6.1%	6.9%	14.22%	11.34%	8.85%	8.39%	8.51%	8.60%	6.31%	8.09%	8.70%	9.10%	7.90%	7.18%
		Washington	2.2%	33.2%	2.7%	1.8%	3.39%	2.96%	2.98%	4.55%	3.39%	2.82%	4.14%	3.32%	3.39%	4.31%	4.18%	5.65%
		Phoenix	7.1%	31.0%	8.9%	8.4%	10.64%	12.39%	10.59%	11.54%	9.61%	8.11%	8.79%	9.63%	10.59%	11.29%	11.86%	9.49%
		Oregon	2.3%	33.3%	3.7%	3.2%	4.63%	4.25%	4.44%	5.10%	5.27%	5.18%	4.83%	5.72%	5.98%	5.84%	5.80%	5.39%
		Vermont	3.7%	33.5%	4.2%	4.2%	4.51%	8.02%	4.86%	8.94%	4.80%	6.95%	7.62%	5.57%	4.79%	5.85%	6.20%	6.43%
		North Dakota	46.9%	47.6%	47.8%	50.0%	60.50%	60.77%	54.61%	46.80%	49.80%	51.73%	48.01%	51.07%	50.74%	53.40%	54.17%	41.87%
		Nevada	0.7%	33.7%	2.2%	1.7%	2.48%	3.20%	3.14%	3.42%	3.34%	3.26%	3.82%	4.38%	4.15%	3.96%	4.77%	4.00%
		Total	1.8%	1.3%	2.1%	2.0%	3.73%	3.90%	3.84%	3.98%	3.76%	3.85%	3.96%	4.07%	3.98%	4.12%	4.15%	4.17%
		New York	1.5%	0.9%	1.9%	1.8%	3.43%	3.71%	3.47%	3.89%	3.64%	3.81%	4.38%	3.75%	4.22%	3.91%	3.90%	3.94%
		Texas	1.7%	1.1%	2.4%	2.1%	3.77%	3.93%	3.85%	3.93%	4.09%	3.98%	4.16%	4.26%	4.08%	4.37%	4.46%	4.29%
		Idaho	1.9%	1.4%	1.1%	1.2%	3.48%	3.00%	3.44%	3.18%	2.70%	3.17%	3.28%	3.17%	3.24%	3.31%	3.17%	2.94%

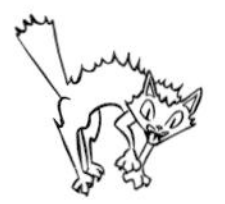

FIGURE 9.27 Original attempt to present top-level KPIs (Voyant Data).

green, some yellow, some red, and a ridiculous number of... numbers. It hurts me to even think of trying to parse this and glean insights.

The Improved Version

Here's a snapshot of the improved version on a particular day and time (Figure 9.28).

We see some blue (good), yellow (of concern), and red (bad), but we also see these within a context of more than just one day. Consider User Loss KPI (1). We see that it had been below the 1.0 percent threshold for 12 months, but only ran into a problem this month. Clicking this KPI will allow the user to drill down to see what may have caused the problem (Figure 9.29).

Here we see a zoomed in trend line (1). Since some KPIs should be below a threshold and others above, the dashboard designer displays light pink bands. If the line is within these bands, there is a problem.

The bar chart on the top left (2) indicates that the problem is just for the most recent period as the three-month average and year-to-date (YTD) average are below threshold (albeit,

FIGURE 9.28 Even at the highest level, we can see KPIs over time and not just this period (Voyant Data).

FIGURE 9.29 Exploring the particulars of the User Loss KPI (Voyant Data).

not as good as the same period in the previous year). And just where is the biggest problem?

Nevada (3), although there are problems with Vermont and Georgia for this month, too. We can also see the 13-month trend for Nevada in the sparkline chart (4), showing that this is the second time in the past 13 months that Nevada has had a problem with this KPI (the line encroaches into the pink area twice).

So, just where in Nevada is the organization having a problem? Clicking the plus sign (+) will allow us to explore all the facilities in that state (Figure 9.30).

Just Because It's Blue Doesn't Mean All Is Well

Figure 9.31 shows a different path a stakeholder might take. Here the dashboard has been filtered to show just Washington State (1), the territory for which the stakeholder is responsible. Notice the User Loss KPI (2). It's blue, but there is a warning icon. Indeed, we can see that the line has spent a fair amount of time above the KPI threshold.

Clicking this KPI displays the User Loss dashboard (Figure 9.32).

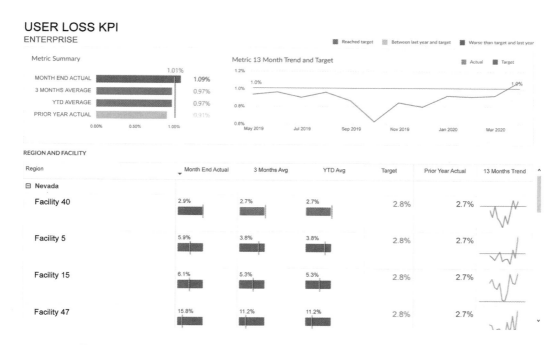

FIGURE 9.30 Exploring user loss by facilities in Nevada (Voyant Data).

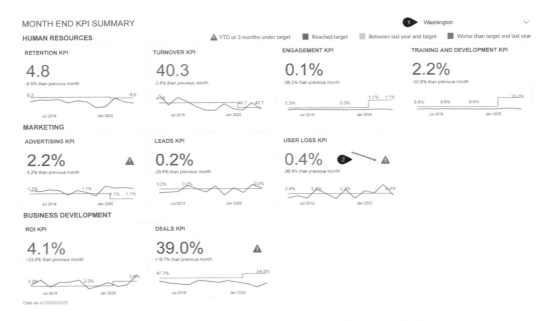

FIGURE 9.31 While the current values for User Loss KPI are good (below threshold) the warning icon indicates there's something worth investigating (Voyant Data).

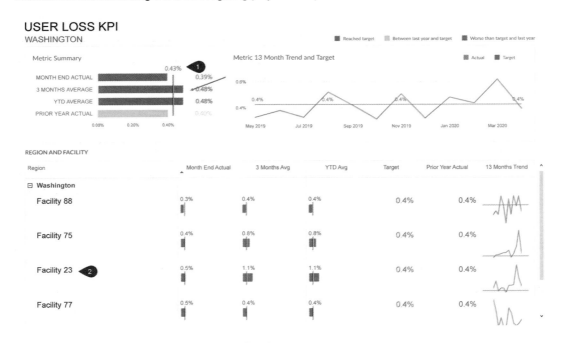

FIGURE 9.32 Details for User Loss KPI (Voyant Data).

Here we see that while the month end for User Loss is below threshold, the three-month average and YTD average are both above the target. We can also see that Facility 23 (2) is especially problematic.

The Impact

The users of the original dashboard struggled with trying to understand why they were under or over target for a specific KPI. They would export data to Excel and build their own ad-hoc reports and analysis. This could take days!

Another frustration was cognitive load; it was just too much on a single screen.

The new dashboard was an instant success. Stakeholders appreciated the clarity in being able to instantly see what areas needed attention (red tiles) within their groups. They could spot early on if their KPIs were starting to trend in the wrong direction by seeing patterns in the time series data.

The overall time savings for business executives has been massive. The dashboard allows them to spend more time actually fixing problems than trying to figure out where the problems are.

Nick Snapp did a particularly good job of not just showing current KPIs but also compressing a 13-month longitudinal view into a compact area. Only showing the current period versus a previous period masks a lot of important information, kind of like looking at a painting through a toilet paper tube. Also noteworthy is how the target line changes as the

organization adjusts its targets during the year (Figure 9.33).

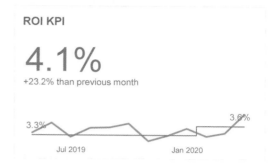

FIGURE 9.33 Target line jumps from 3.3 percent to 3.6 percent as the organization adjusts its goals (Voyant Data).

EXAMPLES OF "SHOCK AND AWE"

Here are three cases of how a simple visualization completely changed perspectives and behavior.

How Do I Get from Raleigh-Durham to Seattle?

Several years ago, the revenue management team at a major airline tasked Nelson Davis, founding partner at Analytic Vizion, with helping the airline understand market performance (a market is defined as a pair of cities between which passengers travel). In this example, Davis was asked to streamline the analysis of seeing how people traveled from Raleigh-Durham to

Seattle, given that the airline did not offer direct flights between the two cities.

Prior to Davis's arrival, the process involved printing five 11-by-17 spreadsheets and manually comparing numbers on one sheet with numbers on other sheets. The airline wanted Davis to fashion a dashboard where all the numbers were in one place.

While having everything in one place would be an improvement, why not try to visualize the data? For example, why not visualize how the network was being utilized by passengers flying between Raleigh-Durham and Seattle?

Apparently, the airline had tried that, and it didn't help anyone understand the data better because people already knew where the cities were on a map.

Davis built what was a giant collection of cross tabs, a portion of which is shown in Figure 9.34.

While having everything in once place (versus five 11-by-17 printouts) was a big improvement, it's still hard to glean insights from a table

Flows by Path - Top 10

	Rev	Pax	Avg
ATL	527K	1,340	393
DTW	190K	502	378
MSP	132K	338	391
JFK	25K	102	249
CVG	28K	90	312
LAX	4K	8	588
ATLSJC	0K	2	161
JFKLAX	0K	2	213
SJC	0K	2	96

Leg Details

Leg Seg	Date	CY Rev	CY Leg Pax	Avg Fare	ASM Y/Y %	Avg HR CY	HR Y/Y $ Δ	RPM Y/Y%	Final LF PY
ATLRDU	12/15	396K	2,086	190	9%	$195	$35	-4%	84%
	01/16	328K	2,318	142	16%	$41	($25)	3%	80%
	02/16	31K	276	112	16%	$50	$0	15%	84%
ATLSEA	12/15	396K	2,086	190	17%	$279	($293)	-4%	99%
	01/16	328K	2,318	142	23%	$209	($90)	3%	98%
	02/16	31K	276	112	29%	$157	($2)	3%	101%
ATLSJC	01/16	0K	4	107	29%	$131	($56)	19%	95%
	02/16	0K	2	178	36%	$150	($17)	81%	96%
CVGRDU	12/15	396K	2,086	190	7%	$218	$42	9%	67%
	01/16	328K	2,318	142	0%	$45	($22)	-20%	72%
	02/16	31K	276	112	67%	$38	($23)	45%	76%
CVGSEA	12/15	396K	2,086	190	35%	$188	($271)	5%	101%
	01/16	328K	2,318	142	8%	$155	($291)	-11%	98%
DTWRDU	12/15	396K	2,086	190	17%	$200	($69)	6%	78%
	01/16	328K	2,318	142	20%	$67	($33)	-8%	72%
	02/16	31K	276	112	16%	$56	($4)	4%	72%
DTWSEA	12/15	396K	2,086	190	20%	$284	($316)	4%	98%
	01/16	328K	2,318	142	12%	$137	($74)	-4%	95%
	02/16	31K	276	112	12%	$120	($23)	-5%	100%
JFKLAX	01/16	0K	4	107	19%	$162	($58)	21%	80%
	02/16	0K	2	178	21%	$85	($41)	19%	86%
JFKRDU	12/15	396K	2,086	190	38%	$206	$7	29%	86%
	01/16	328K	2,318	142	52%	$54	($31)	33%	74%
	02/16	31K	276	112	43%	$41	($18)	15%	75%
JFKSEA	12/15	396K	2,086	190	26%	$290	($319)	3%	98%
	01/16	328K	2,318	142	22%	$127	($117)	-1%	89%
	02/16	31K	276	112	26%	$89	($51)	4%	92%
LAXRDU	12/15	396K	2,086	190	15%	$290	($235)	-10%	97%
	01/16	328K	2,318	142	24%	$108	($48)	7%	84%
	02/16	31K	276	112	9%	$54	$14	26%	88%
LAXSEA	12/15	396K	2,086	190	43%	$266	($69)	20%	90%
	01/16	328K	2,318	142	52%	$69	($43)	24%	77%
	02/16	31K	276	112	30%	$97	($34)	2%	83%
MSPRDU	12/15	396K	2,086	190	10%	$200	($60)	-4%	80%
	01/16	328K	2,318	142	11%	$75	($52)	-5%	77%
	02/16	31K	276	112	14%	$61	($24)	-16%	79%
MSPSEA	12/15	396K	2,086	190	14%	$257	($201)	-7%	97%
	01/16	328K	2,318	142	12%	$152	($78)	-10%	96%
	02/16	31K	276	112	15%	$122	($15)	-16%	98%
SEASJC	01/16	0K	4	107	9%	$38	$5	-6%	66%
	02/16	0K	2	178	12%	$51	$29	-30%	73%

FIGURE 9.34 A segment of a collection of cross tabs showing market performance for Raleigh-Durham and Seattle (Nelson Davis).

full of numbers. Undaunted, Davis decided to build a map and add it to the dashboard.

But not just any map. Davis built a flow map (Figure 9.35).

Yes! The very same type of map Minard used in his Russian Campaign visualization (Chapter 8).

The client was completely floored by this. They had never really had a visceral understanding for just how much revenue was generated by the Atlanta-Seattle segment, the longest and thickest line on the map.

The impact went beyond the revenue management team as the flow map was shared with other departments, all of which had similar reactions. It wasn't that Davis had discovered new numbers—everyone knew the numbers—it was that until people saw the flow map, they didn't really see and feel the impact of these numbers.

The organization rewarded Davis's initiative by asking him to replicate the same flow map analysis for all markets (city pairs) in the airline's network.

In this case, just one new chart made a difference and had a massive impact.

Flow Map Network (Raleigh Durham and Seattle)

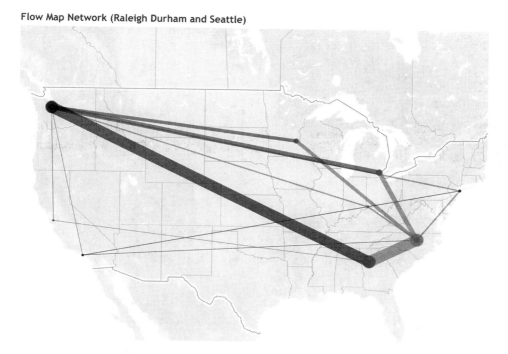

FIGURE 9.35 A flow map showing revenue generated between various cities (Nelson Davis).

Understanding Partner Stratification

Note: the data in this example is not real but is suggestive of the actual data and is representative of what you would see in many organizations.

Several years ago, Greg Lewandowski, currently the Director of Process Improvement in the WW Partner Organization at Citrix Systems, Inc., was working with a major global technology provider to understand the organization's partner relationships. The organization had over 25,000 different partners, and Lewandowski and his colleagues were frustrated by requests to look at the top 25 partners or the top 50 partners, as these numbers seemed arbitrary.

Ranking the customers from highest to lowest revenue producers, Lewandowski proposed putting the customers into different segments, as follows:

- Of the top ranked partners, how many are responsible for 25 percent of sales?

- Of the next ranked, how many are responsible for 26–50 percent of sales?

I'll confess that when Lewandowski presented this to me, I thought he was going to present a classic 80/20 Pareto analysis in which 20 percent of the partners would be responsible for 80 percent of the revenue.

This was not the case. Figure 9.36 shows the initial analysis showing the tiers and how many partners fell into each tier.

Partner Stratification Analysis

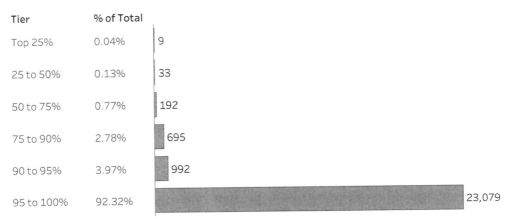

Tier	% of Total	
Top 25%	0.04%	9
25 to 50%	0.13%	33
50 to 75%	0.77%	192
75 to 90%	2.78%	695
90 to 95%	3.97%	992
95 to 100%	92.32%	23,079

FIGURE 9.36 A bar chart showing the breakdown by different tiers. I usually advise against showing two decimal places because it adds clutter, but in this case, the data warrants that level of precision (Greg Lewandowski).

Some quick mental arithmetic shows that roughly 1 percent of the partners are responsible for 75 percent of the revenue!

In any case, this is not what Lewandowski shared with his decision-making colleagues.

Knowing his audience, he started by showing just what 25,000 partners looks like (Figure 9.37).

Figure 9.38 shows the top partners that are responsible for 25 percent of revenue.

Imagine each dot is a partner. There are 25,000 dots.

FIGURE 9.37 So that's what 25,000 items looks like (Greg Lewandowski).

These partners are responsible for 25% of our sales.

FIGURE 9.38 Nine partners are responsible for 25 percent of revenue (Greg Lewandowski).

Figure 9.39 shows the top partners that are responsible for 75 percent of revenue.

Lewandowski called this the "jawbreaker" because of the sound made when so many jaws dropped and hit the floor. Like all good visualizations, it not only answered questions, it spawned some great ones, including an analysis of partners that had moved from the lower tiers to the top tier: What was special about those partners? What could the organization do to nurture more partners like those?

These partners **are responsible for** 75% of our sales.

FIGURE 9.39 Two hundred thirty-four partners are responsible for 75 percent of revenue (Greg Lewandowski).

If asked, "How many times out of 100 should you use a bar chart or line chart instead of something eye-catching?" I would respond, "99." So why am I sharing an example that celebrates the packed bubbles that I dismissed in Chapter 1? In this case, the bubbles are very effective because we don't need to make accurate comparisons. It's not important to be able to see that the biggest bar is 2,564 times as large as the smallest bar versus only 2,400 times as large. The big picture is that a tiny fraction of partners is responsible for a massive amount of revenue.

Resource Planning

What follows is a repurposing of a real-world example that saved an organization millions of dollars. The person who created the visualization is not able to share the details, but the simple dashboard was so striking and made such a big difference that I rebuilt it and created a similar type of use case.

Individual departments within an organization are convinced that they don't have nearly enough conference rooms to keep up with demand, and they want the organization to build new conference rooms. Although the organization can use any conference room, each department has its own allocation and is responsible for meeting its own needs first and then opening their siloed rooms to others.

The organization hires a space-allocation expert who tells the department heads that they have plenty of space and if they were to use a centralized allocation system, they would be able to fulfill conference room needs without investing in new space.

Nobody believes the consultant. They are convinced that their feel for the situation is correct. The consultant responds with a powerful pair of visualizations showing that the organization is in fact way under capacity and that if they were to move to a centralized approach, they would be able to meet demand and not strain capacity. Here are the two paired charts that left mouths agape. Note that the goal is to be at 65 percent utilization or higher.

Figure 9.40 shows the day and hour conference room use, applying the "seat of our pants" approach to scheduling.

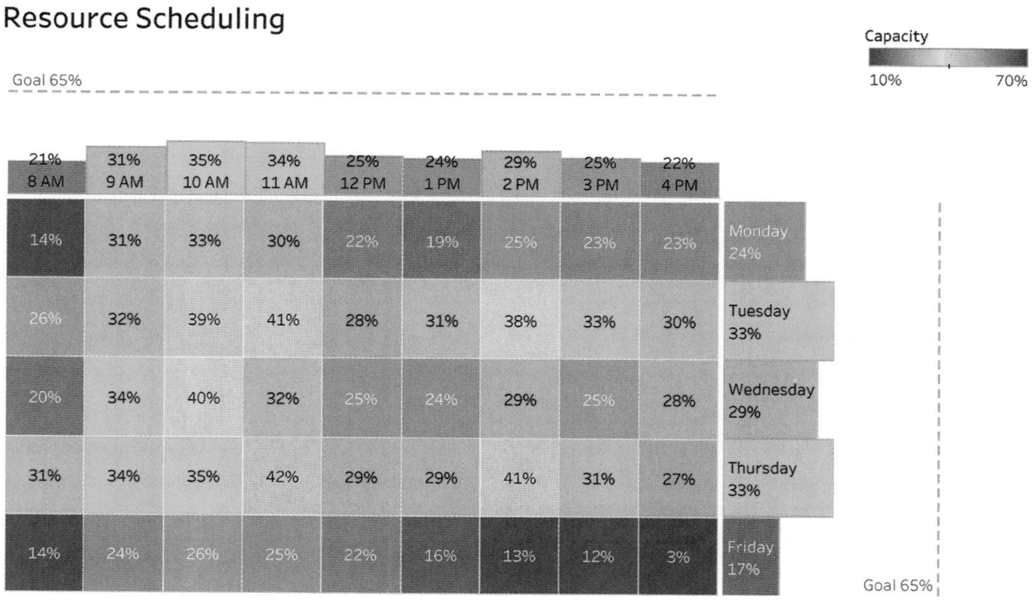

Resource Scheduling

FIGURE 9.40 A highlight table with marginal histograms. Everything is well below the goal of 65 percent capacity.

Figure 9.41 shows what the resource allocation would look like with a centralized approach.

The centralized approach yields much better results except for 4 PM on Friday (1), And really, who wants to have a meeting at 4 PM on a Friday?

These paired visualizations had a monumental influence on the organization. For whatever reasons, stakeholders did not believe the thesis about resource utilization until they saw it presented in a compelling visualization.

OH, THE POSSIBILITIES WHEN YOU ARE A "POSSIBILIST"

Hans Rosling was a Swedish professor of global health who, using data, stunning visualizations, and homespun charm, changed the way people understood the world.

I first became aware of his work when a friend showed me Rosling's TED Talk from 2006. If you haven't seen it, I encourage you to watch it (see bigpic.me/rosling).

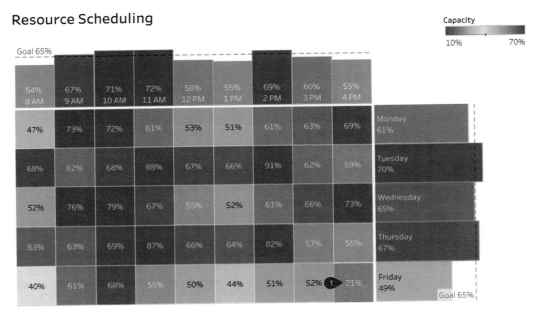

FIGURE 9.41 A highlight table with marginal histograms using a centralized approach.

Rosling was a true pioneer in using data—in particular, visualizing data—to help correct peoples' misperceptions about the world. He didn't set out to be a visualization visionary; he just realized that he needed to create new techniques so people would be able to better see and understand the world. As he states in another of his videos, "Having the data is not enough. I have to show it in ways people both enjoy and understand."

In his book *Factfulness: Ten Reasons We're Wrong About the World—and Why Things Are Better Than You Think*, Rosling describes himself as a "possibilist":

People often call me an optimist, because I show them the enormous progress they didn't know about. That makes me angry. I'm not an optimist. That makes me sound naïve. I'm a very serious "possibilist." That's something I made up. It means someone who neither hopes without reason, nor fears without reason, someone who constantly resists the overdramatic worldview. As a possibilist, I see all this progress, and it fills me with conviction and hope that further progress is possible. This is not optimistic. It is having a clear and reasonable idea about how things are. It is having a worldview that is constructive and useful.*

Here are examples from three "possibilists" who have ideas about how much clearer and more useful data could be if it were presented in a way that people both "enjoy and understand."

Reimagining the Profit and Loss Statement

Klaus Schulte is a professor at the Münster School of Business, where he teaches financial and management accounting. He's also a pioneer in data visualization and shares a frustration with accountants' reluctance to embrace visualization. He decided to take on the standard, decades-old profit-and-loss (P&L) statement and make it more accessible; however, he did not have the accountants in mind (although he'd love to win them over, too). The goal was to help people not steeped in standard accounting reports, so they could better understand accounting data.

Figure 9.42 shows Alphabet Inc.'s P&L statement from 2019. Alphabet is the parent company of Google.

This looks a lot like the examples from the beginning of the book.

Figure 9.43 shows Schulte's reimagining.

So many elements buried in the table of numbers pop out. For example, look at the sources of revenue along the right (marked as

---

* Rosling, Hans. *Factfulness* (New York: Flatiron Books, 2018), Kindle edition, 69.

Alphabet Inc.
CONSOLIDATED STATEMENTS OF INCOME

(In millions, except per share amounts)	Year Ended December 31, 2017	2018	2019
Revenues	$ 110,855	$ 136,819	$ 161,857
Costs and expenses:			
Cost of revenues	45,583	59,549	71,896
Research and development	16,625	21,419	26,018
Sales and marketing	12,893	16,333	18,464
General and administrative	6,840	6,923	9,551
European Commission fines	2,736	5,071	1,697
Total costs and expenses	84,677	109,295	127,626
Income from operations	26,178	27,524	34,231
Other income (expense), net	1,015	7,389	5,394
Income before income taxes	27,193	34,913	39,625
Provision for income taxes	14,531	4,177	5,282
Net income	$ 12,662	$ 30,736	$ 34,343
Basic net income per share of Class A and B common stock and Class C capital stock	$ 18.27	$ 44.22	$ 49.59
Diluted net income per share of Class A and B common stock and Class C capital stock	$ 18.00	$ 43.70	$ 49.16

See accompanying notes.

FIGURE 9.42 Alphabet Inc. P&L statement from 2019 (Alphabet, Inc. 2019 annual report).

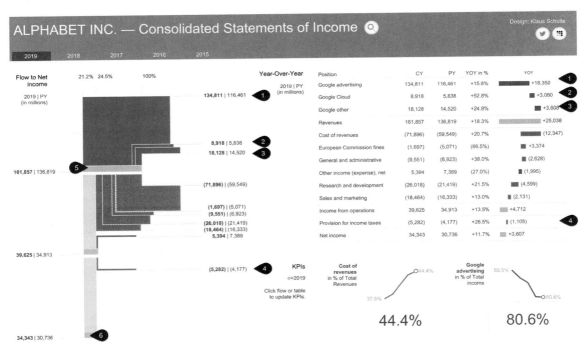

FIGURE 9.43 Schulte's approach to presenting P&L data. Notice that the table of numbers is preserved but has been buttressed with visualizations to emphasize the year-over-year change within the table and to show the magnitude of those numbers and the flow in and out of the organization (Klaus Schulte).

(1), (2), and (3)) and see how they correspond to the matched inflow elements in the flow diagram along the left.

Compare also the Provision for Income Taxes along the right (4) with the corresponding outflow element in the chart on the left.

Finally, note the length of the overall revenue (5) with the net profit (6). Goodness, Alphabet Inc. was profitable in 2019.

The KPI card on the bottom right shows relative values and change over time, additional information not included in traditional P&L statements.

Reimagining Lab Tests

Amanda Makulec is a Senior Data Visualization Lead at Excella and Operations Director at the Data Visualization Society. After her father had a second battle against kidney cancer, Makulec decided that she should submit to a genetic test and discovered that she, like her father, had Lynch syndrome, which put her at greater risk

for several different types of cancers. The lab results she received were presented in a table like the one shown in Figure 9.44.

Lots of body parts, lots of numbers, and lots of red—and a lot of frustration with the way the data was presented.

It's hard not to be particularly alarmed by the first set of numbers (55–82 percent) and just focus on the 82 percent, suggesting there is a four out of five risk of that body part developing cancer.

Armed with both a master's degree in public health and data visualization expertise, Makulec could interpret the results but wondered about those not as well steeped in reading and understanding health-related numbers. She wished the testing company had presented the results this way instead (Figure 9.45).

If you are wondering why there is a dot for the general population and a very wide range for Makulec, it's because of the amount of data the testing organization maintains. They have a great deal of data about the general population

CANCER TYPE	CANCER RISK	POPULATION RISK	RELATED TO
BODY PART			
To age xx	55%-82%	1.9%	GENE MUTATION YOU HAVE
BODY PART			
To age xx	51%-68%	2.5%	GENE MUTATION YOU HAVE
BODY PART			
To age xx	40%-64%	4.5%	GENE MUTATION YOU HAVE
BODY PART			
To age xx	30%-41%	1.2%	GENE MUTATION YOU HAVE
BODY PART			
To age xx	11%-38%	1.3%	GENE MUTATION YOU HAVE
BODY PART			

FIGURE 9.44 A portion of Makulec's test results (Amanda Makulec).

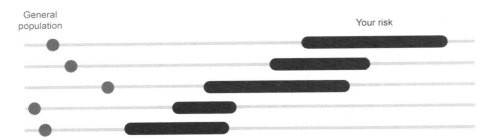

General population

Your risk

FIGURE 9.45 Makulec's lab results visualized showing range bars (Amanda Makulec).

but sparse data from people with Lynch syndrome, so the margin of error is very wide, hence the wide range bars.

Reimagining Health Histories

It can be overwhelming for people with rare, mysterious, or complicated health issues to relate their health histories to doctors. At appointments, people feel pressured to remember what happened and tell their story in the right order. The details are often trapped in old medical records. It's challenging to tell your entire history, especially when visiting a new doctor. It's also exhausting. With each new doctor, the patient has to start from scratch, and the details often get lost in translation. And many patients feel they are not being taken seriously, or they are told that their symptoms are all in their head.

Katie McCurdy, founder of Pictal Health, offers a health history visualization service to help patients organize and visualize their health histories so they can understand what happened, communicate better, and tell their stories

with confidence. An example is shown in Figure 9.46.

After carefully interviewing patients, McCurdy makes these visuals individually and provides a copy for the patient to take to their next appointment. These customized visualizations provide doctors with information they want and need—such as past diagnoses, injuries and illnesses, and surgeries—in a format that is much easier to see and parse than what's in standard medical records. They also incorporate helpful information that can only come from the patient, such as symptom history, life events, non-medication treatments, and lifestyle changes. The result is a holistic view that (a) helps patients better understand their own histories and advocate for themselves; and (b) gives doctors the information they need to make better diagnostic and treatment recommendations.

The results for the 50+ patients for whom McCurdy has visualized health histories have been very encouraging. Patients armed with these visualizations recount that they are not just being seen by doctors—they are being heard.

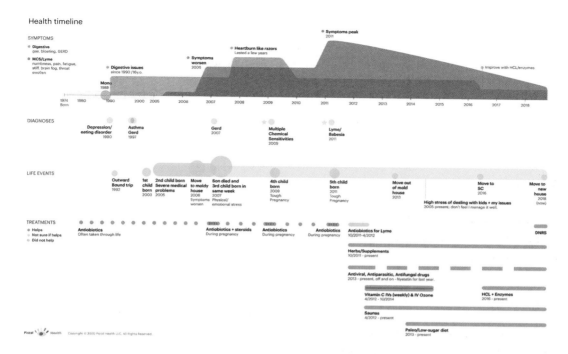

FIGURE 9.46 A patient's health history visualized (Katie McCurdy, Pictal Health).

One patient said, "I can't tell you how much seeing this completed means to me. I honestly broke down and cried because I felt so seen in a way I haven't for a while now."

Another confirmed, "The visuals helped the doctor focus on the most important symptoms and understand which classes of drugs worked or didn't work. And he spent A LOT less time in the computer system and A LOT more time brainstorming ideas for a future treatment plan."

MY STORY

If you visit my "About" page, you'll see that my degrees are in music. My passion was for jazz, Broadway, and the Beatles, and my expertise was in arranging and orchestration. I also play electric bass.

My music endeavors were mostly dormant for over a dozen years when, in 2004, a good friend encouraged me to watch the documentary *Standing in the Shadows of Motown*. This is the story of The Funk Brothers, the Motown backup band that played on more number-one records than the Beatles, the Rolling Stones, and Elvis Presley combined.

The movie knocked me out, and I decided all I wanted to do was play soul and R&B. I became obsessed with James Jamerson, the bassist who laid down killer grooves for The Four Tops,

Marvin Gaye, Stevie Wonder, Gladys Knight—you get the picture. I was determined to learn his basslines, and I started woodshedding.

In 2005, I got hired to play with a very good local R&B band. This would be my first time playing soul and R&B in public, and I was excited. And nervous.

I managed not to screw up in the first set. As for the second set, something amazing happened. We opened with the song "My Girl," which starts with an immediately recognizable solo bassline.* I played all of six notes, and people jumped up and filled the dance floor.

Holy s&*t! I couldn't believe it. I just played six notes and people went nuts. I *literally* moved people.

I wanted to experience that again and again and again.

Fast-forward to 2013. I had the good fortune to work with a major healthcare company. They had data from thousands of organizations about millions of employees and were working on a campaign.

Yes, you guessed it, this is the story behind the example about the incidence of diabetes (see the Introduction). It was the first time I saw an audience have a visceral reaction to a data visualization I helped build. I *figuratively* moved people.

I want to experience that again and again and again.

YOUR STORY

If you are someone who creates charts and dashboards, you can make a difference within your organization. Just think of the position you are in: you have the ability to create *aha* moments every time you fashion a data visualization. Once this happens, you'll be hooked! And you'll soon be teaching others how to do it. It's insanely fulfilling.

If you are someone who consumes the work of others, you may be wondering what you can do. Of course, if you are a senior executive with clout, then you can mandate change (you can also order a copy of this book for everyone in your organization).

But what if you are not a senior executive who can easily put the gears into motion? What can you do?

You can share what you've learned with others. When you see a table full of numbers or a scaredy-cat of a visualization, you can get others excited about presenting the data differently. I'd wager there are examples in this book that you can apply to situations in your own workplace. Show colleagues what they are missing!

You can also learn to do this, right now or at any point in your career. I am a poster child for this as I got started in my mid-forties, and I created *many* scaredy-cat visualizations. But I learned. The data visualization community is very nurturing, and its practitioners are very generous with their time. Join us!

---

* You know how it goes . . . "Bah-DAH-dah. Bah-DAH-dah. Bah-DAH-dah. Bah-DAH-dah." Then the guitar comes in.

WHERE TO GO FROM HERE

I've talked about the importance of collaboration in developing great data visualizations. To help you get others excited, here's a link to a synopsis of key points in the book and a few of the most eye-opening charts in an easy-to-share format: bigpic.me/jumpstart.

If you'd like to be more than just an informed consumer of charts—someone who helps drive change through data visualization—here are some valuable resources.

BOOKS

How Charts Lie: Getting Smarter about Visual Information by Alberto Cairo. To get an understanding of how charts can both inform and mislead, read this book. Cairo is concerned about how politicians, advertisers, and the media use charts to bamboozle the public. He desperately wants to stop the spread of misinformation and wants you, the reader, to know BS when you see it. As he writes, "We all have the civic duty to avoid spreading charts and stories that may be misleading. We must contribute to a healthier informational environment."

Factfulness: Ten Reasons We're Wrong About the World—and Why Things Are Better Than You Think by Hans Rosling. Rosling was an expert on global health, a data visualization pioneer, and an expert teacher and storyteller. He was also desperate to remedy people's misconceptions about the world, which he would do with data combined with clear and compelling graphics. Rosling will challenge your worldview and likely make you feel better about our lot.

The Data Detective: Ten Easy Rules to Make Sense of Statistics by Tim Harford. Harford is a senior columnist at the *Financial Times* and hosts a popular BBC program in the UK. In this terrific complement to *How Charts Lie* and *Factfulness*, Harford shows how preconceptions and biases lead us astray, clouding our ability to make rational decisions. Harford shows where and how this happens, and what you can do to combat it.

Avoiding Data Pitfalls: How to Steer Clear of Common Blunders When Working with Data and Presenting Analysis and Visualizations by Ben Jones. Data visualizations can do great harm if the data upon which they are built is not accurate and complete. Jones, a champion of data literacy, will help you steer clear of the myriad stumbling blocks and pitfalls that can sabotage your decision-making efforts.

Storytelling with Data: A Data Visualization Guide for Business Professionals by Cole Nussbaumer Knaflic. Geared toward the people who create charts, Knaflic teaches data communicators how to take cluttered and confusing graphics and turn them into clear and compelling narratives that inform and engage.

The Big Book of Dashboards: Visualizing Your Data Using Real-World Business Scenarios by Steve Wexler, Jeffrey Shaffer, and Andy Cotgreave. This book is for those seeking examples and inspiration from various organizations that have built solid dashboard solutions to typical business and organizational problems.

TOOLS

This book and all the books listed in this section are tool agnostic. The books will help you learn what you should do and why you should do it, but they won't discuss the particulars of how to build something using a specific tool.

There are some great tools that can help you build what you want to build, faster. Here is a partial list:

- Tableau, from Tableau Software (a Salesforce company)
- Microsoft Excel, from Microsoft
- Microsoft Power BI, from Microsoft
- QlikView and Qlik Sense, from Qlik
- MicroStrategy, from MicroStrategy
- Looker, from Google
- Juicebox, from Juice Analytics
- Dundas BI, from Dundas
- Spotfire, from Tibco

ORGANIZATIONS

Join the Data Visualization Society, which aims to collect and establish best practices, and fosters a community that supports members as they grow and develop data visualization skills. See www.datavisualizationsociety.com.

BIG PICTURE EXTRAS

For videos, resources, additional examples, and free downloads, please visit bigpic.me/extras.

ACKNOWLEDGMENTS

I want to extend a long overdue thank-you to David Holcombe and Heidi Fisk, the founders of The Learning Guild and the people who gave me my start in data visualization. The world is now ready for the system we tried to put together all those years ago. Along with David and Heidi, I need to thank Marc Rueter from Tableau, who patiently guided me during my data visualization infancy.

I am deeply indebted to Elissa Fink, who recommended me for my first solo practitioner data visualization gig. I desperately needed that first job and I don't think I would be here without her backing.

I am grateful to my clients and workshop attendees who challenged my assertions and asked good questions. It was these challenges and questions that inspired me to write this book, and I hope it will help them evangelize data visualization within their organizations.

I asked several colleagues to be my "deep readers" and review the full draft manuscript.

Andy Cotgreave, Kendall Crolius, Dalton Ruer, and Cole Nussbaumer Knaflic all provided insanely useful feedback. They made my life a little more difficult, but they made the book a whole lot better.

Over the two years I worked on this project I asked many friends and colleagues to review sections and to bounce around ideas. A big thank-you to RJ Andrews, Zach Bowders, Simon Beaumont, Anthony Brown, Chad Skelton, Jeffrey Shaffer, Amanda Makulec, Sue Kraemer, Randy Krum, Ben Jones, John Pittenger, Marina Brazhnikova, Brodie Dore, Elissa Fink, Elizabeth Ricks, Alberto Cairo, Mark Jackson, Allen Jackson, Daniel Zvinca, Josh Tapley, Jon Schwabish, Nigel Henry, Reuben Shorser, Matt Rush, Troy Magennis, Jorge Camoes, Leslie Lee Fook, Egbert Irving, Curtis Harris, Allen Hillery, and Jason Forrest for your encouragement of the good and the gentle discouraging of the not-so-good.

My deep thanks to the many people who contributed stellar examples, including Dorian Banutoiu, Lindsay Betzendahl, Cole Nussbaumer Knaflic, Hesham Eissa, Simon Beaumont, Chris Lay, Nick Snapp, Nelson Davis, Greg Lewandowski, Klaus Schulte, Amanda Makulec, Katie McCurdy, Curtis Harris, Jenn Schilling, and Matt Chambers.

Joe Mako helped guide me through many thorny data visualization challenges over the years, and did more than anyone to establish the ethos of the Tableau community.

Stephen Few sent me down the right path with his wonderful books *Show Me the Numbers* and *Now You See It*. If he reads this book, I hope he doesn't think I've veered from that path.

My agent, David Fugate, helped me find a great home for the book at McGraw Hill with editor Casey Ebro, who was quick to give others credit when things went well (I'm thinking of you, Jonathan Sperling, who came up with the book title) and was quick to take the blame when there were problems—if only our political leaders were like this! Casey, thank you for the invaluable feedback and edits, and for assembling a great team, including art director Jeff Weeks and copy editor (and trusted advisor) Christina Verigan.

Mauna Eichner and Lee Fukui, who managed the design, composition, and production, it was wonderful having you in my corner.

My Chart Chat colleagues, Amanda Makulec, Andy Cotgreave, and Jeffrey Shaffer, set such a high bar for delivering fun and engaging content (and an extra deep bow to Andy and Jeff for the content I'm referencing from *The Big Book of Dashboards*).

An additional thank-you to Jeff for helping me take the plunge into presenting workshops before I thought I was ready. Without Jeff it would have taken much longer, and the content would not be as good.

To my gym breakfast Zoom buddies, Patricia Moro, Joyce Lannert, Lloyd Newman, Herb and Dale Schuman, Jay and Sue Castle, Mike Cook, Harriette DeCarlo, and Rob Schrader: our 200+ morning Zoom meetings made me laugh and helped keep me sane while I was writing this book during the pandemic.

My dear friends Brad Epstein and Ira Handler who both provided great examples and who make me better, simply by being around them.

To my daughters, Janine and Diana, the craziness of the pandemic meant I got to spend much more time with you than I would have otherwise. I am grateful for this gift.

And to my wife and best friend, Laura, who from book inception to delivery has provided advice, encouragement, comic relief—and really good proofreading!

INDEX

ABOUT THE AUTHOR

Steve Wexler is the founder of Data Revelations, a data visualization consultancy. He has worked with ADP, Gallup, Johnson & Johnson, Deloitte, ExxonMobil, Tableau Software, Microsoft, Convergys, Bayer, Disney, *Consumer Reports*, *The Economist*, SurveyMonkey, Con Edison, D&B, Marist College, Cornell University, Stanford University, Tradeweb, Tiffany, McKinsey & Company, and many other organizations to help them understand and visualize their data. A winner of numerous data visualization honors and awards, Steve also serves on the advisory board of the Data Visualization Society. His presentations and workshops combine an extraordinary level of product mastery with real-world experience gained through developing thousands of visualizations for clients. Steve has taught tens of thousands of people in both large and small organizations.

He is the coauthor of *The Big Book of Dashboards: Visualizing Your Data Using Real-World Business Scenarios*.

For more information, please visit datarevelations.com.